M000202074

Canada Dry® Alcohol-Free Party Drinks

Canada Dry® Alcohol-Free Party Drinks

Compiled by Shelley Kilander Logan

The Summit Publishing Group
Arlington, Texas

THE SUMMIT PUBLISHING GROUP
One Arlington Centre, 1112 East Copeland Road, Fifth Floor
Arlington, Texas 76011
summit@dfw.net
www.summitbooks.com

Copyright © 1997 Dr Pepper/Seven Up, Inc.
All rights reserved. No part of this book may be reproduced or trans-
mitted in any form or by any means, electronic or mechanical,
including photocopying, recording, or by any information storage
and retrieval system, without the written permission of the publisher,
except where permitted by law.

Printed in the United States of America.

01 00 99 98 97   5 4 3 2 1

Canada dry alcohol-free party drinks / edited by Shelley Kilander
    Logan.
        p.   cm.
     ISBN 1-56530-272-9 (pbk.)
     1. Beverages.   I. Logan, Shelley Kilander, 1974-   .
    TX815.C29 1997
    641.8'75—dc21   97-33782
                                                         CIP

Cover design by Dennis Davidson
Book design by John Baird
Layout by Creative Fuel, Fort Worth, Texas
Illustrations by Shelley Kilander Logan

CONTENTS

INTRODUCTION

You're having a party! And you know one of the most important elements of a successful get-together is the drinks. After all, what are your guests cradling in their hands while they are mingling, munching, milling, and merry-making? A glass of one of your luscious libations!

Today's affairs present hosts and hostesses with two questions: "What do I serve the many people who prefer not to drink alcohol?" and "What can I offer that is more festive than just canned soda and coffee alone?"

We would like to help you with the answers. And not just any answers, but more than 300 delicious, crowd-pleasing non-alcoholic drinks sure to help you pull off the perfect party.

Now you can bring great recipes into your own kitchen. The recipes include Canada Dry, 7 UP, Schweppes, A&W, Sunkist, and other soft drinks, a bountiful harvest of other wonderful ingredients such as juice, fruit, ice, and more. You can create drinks that will make the occasion and make *you* a hero.

Cheers!

CHAPTER

1

Slushy Treats

When the summer heats up, everyone likes to cool down with a favorite icy treat. With a blender and just a few simple ingredients, these slushy favorites are a quick way to escape the heat. Pick your favorites, mix, blend, and enjoy.

Cafe Au Lait Freeze

3 cups coffee
2 cups sugar
2 cups half & half
4 cups milk
2 teaspoons vanilla
whipped cream
maraschino cherries

Mix first five ingredients well and freeze for about 4 hours, stirring occasionally. When slushy, serve in parfait glasses. Garnish with whipped cream and a maraschino cherry. Makes 8 servings.

Citrus Slush

1 6-ounce can frozen orange juice concentrate, slightly thawed
1 6-ounce can frozen lemonade concentrate, slightly thawed
2 cups crushed ice
1 teaspoon sugar
2 cups Canada Dry® Club Soda
1 orange, quartered

Blend frozen juices. Add ice and blend until slushy. Add sugar and blend until fluffy. Pour mixture in pitcher and stir in Canada Dry® Club Soda. Serve in chilled wine glasses with orange quarter for garnish. Makes 6 servings.

Canada Dry Ginger Ale Slush

½ cup boiling water
½ cup sugar
1 quart Canada Dry® Ginger Ale
½ cup orange juice
1 small can crushed pineapple with juice
6 whole strawberries

Stir sugar into water until completely dissolved. Combine sugar-water mixture with remaining liquids and pineapple and place in freezer. Stir with whisk about every 45 minutes. When partially frozen, transfer to chilled wine glasses. Garnish with strawberry. Makes 6 servings.

Strawberry-Peach Slush

1 ½ cups peach nectar
1 cup fresh strawberries, quartered
2 teaspoons sugar
½ cup 7 UP®
½ cup crushed ice
strawberry quarters

Combine first five ingredients in blender. Blend until slushy. Serve in chilled parfait glasses and garnish with strawberry quarters. Serves 2.

Frozen Lime Soda

  1 6-ounce can frozen limeade concentrate, slightly
    thawed
  1 6-ounce can frozen pineapple juice, slightly
    thawed
  1 6-ounce can cold water
  ¾ cup Canada Dry® Club Soda
  4 cups ice
  lime slices
  maraschino cherries

Place first five ingredients in blender and mix well.
Garnish with lime slice and cherry. Makes 6 servings.

Grapefruit Freeze

  1 grapefruit
  1 cup sugar
  2 cups water
  juice from 1 lemon
  4 cups Canada Dry® Ginger Ale

Cut grapefruit in half. Squeeze juice from ½ of grapefruit and set aside. Remove fruit from other half. Mix
this half of grapefruit with sugar. Add grapefruit juice,
water, and lemon juice. Mix until thoroughly blended.
Freeze overnight. When ready to serve, scoop into tall
glass and fill with Canada Dry® Ginger Ale. Makes 6
servings.

Blueberry Slush

¼ cup sugar
¾ cup boiling water
6 cups fresh blueberries
1 ½ cups strawberry nectar
¼ cup lemon juice
8 fresh pineapple chunks

Dissolve sugar in water. Combine sugar-water mixture with next three ingredients and blend until smooth. Place ingredients in large bowl and freeze. Whisk about every 40 minutes. When mixture has reached desired consistency, remove and pour into parfait glasses. Garnish each glass with fresh pineapple chunk. Makes 8 servings.

Raspberry Chill

1 cup fresh or frozen raspberries
½ cup nonalcoholic rosé wine
½ cup sour cream
1 cup crushed ice
1 liter Canada Dry® Ginger Ale
fresh raspberries

Combine first four ingredients in blender and blend until smooth. Just before serving, add Canada Dry® Ginger Ale and stir. Serve in chilled wine glasses with floating fresh raspberries for garnish. Makes 8 servings.

Icy Peach Treat

2 fresh peaches, peeled and pitted
½ cup peach nectar
1 cup Canada Dry® Ginger Ale
2 tablespoons lime juice
½ teaspoon grated lime peel
2 tablespoons sugar
2 cups crushed ice
maraschino cherries

Combine first seven ingredients in blender and mix until ice is crushed. Serve in frosty mugs and garnish with maraschino cherries. Makes 2 servings.

Pineapple-Strawberry Slush

2 cups crushed pineapple, with juice
1 10-ounce package frozen strawberries
2 cups crushed ice
fresh strawberries

Combine first three ingredients in blender. Blend about 15 seconds or until slushy. Top with a whole fresh strawberry. Makes 2 large servings.

Old Time Rock 'n Roll Slush

¾ cup sugar
1 cup strong hot tea
1 6-ounce can frozen lemonade concentrate,
    thawed
1 6-ounce can frozen orange juice concentrate,
    thawed
8 cups water
1 2-liter bottle 7 UP®
maraschino cherry
fresh mint sprigs

Dissolve sugar in hot tea. Mix tea with frozen juices in a gallon container. Add water and mix well. Freeze until slushy. Fill glass half full with slush and add 7 UP® to fill glass. Garnish with maraschino cherry and mint sprigs. Makes 20 servings.

Berry Surprise

1 cup frozen raspberries, thawed
½ teaspoon sugar
2 ½ cups MOTT'S® apple juice
1 2-liter bottle Canada Dry® Ginger Ale, chilled
fresh raspberries

Blend frozen berries, sugar, and MOTT'S® apple juice until smooth. Fill glasses half full with mixture and add Canada Dry® Ginger Ale to fill glasses. Garnish with fresh raspberries. Makes 4 servings.

Orange Slush

    1 6-ounce can frozen orange juice concentrate,
        thawed
    1 ½ cups milk
    1 ½ cups water
    ½ cup sugar
    8–10 ice cubes
    maraschino cherries

Blend first five ingredients until smooth (about 30 seconds). Serve immediately in small glasses. Garnish with maraschino cherry. Makes 4 servings.

7UP® Apricot Slush

    2 tea bags
    1 cup boiling water
    ½ cup sugar
    4 cups cold water
    1 6-ounce can frozen orange juice concentrate, thawed
    1 6-ounce can frozen lemonade concentrate, thawed
    1 can apricot nectar
    1 2-liter bottle 7 UP®
    maraschino cherries

Steep tea bags in boiling water about 5 minutes. Add ½ cup sugar to hot tea and stir until dissolved. Combine tea with cold water, juices, and nectar. Place in covered container in freezer. At serving time, fill glasses ¾ full with slush and top with 7 UP®. Garnish with maraschino cherry. Makes 10 servings.

Pineapple Slush

¼ cup sugar

¾ cup boiling water

6 cups fresh pineapple chunks

1 12-ounce can mango nectar

¼ cup lemon juice

8 pineapple chunks

Dissolve sugar in water. Combine sugar-water mixture with next three ingredients and blend until smooth. Place ingredients in large bowl and freeze. Whisk about every 40 minutes. When mixture has reached desired consistency, remove and pour into parfait glasses. Garnish each glass with fresh pineapple chunk. Makes 8 servings.

Famous Amos Blend

3 cups crushed ice

1 cup strawberries, halved

1 cup peach nectar

2 tablespoons sugar

1 cup pineapple juice

2 strawberry halves

Combine first five ingredients in blender. Blend until thoroughly mixed and slushy. Serve immediately in parfait glasses with strawberry halves split on rim of glasses. Makes 2 servings.

Tropical Dream

4 cups ice
1/3 banana, sliced
2 cups pineapple juice
2 cups mango nectar
2 tablespoons cream of coconut
fresh pineapple chunks

Blend first five ingredients until smooth and slushy. Serve immediately in wine glass with fresh pineapple chunks on toothpick. Makes 2 servings.

Fruit Cooler

2 cups ice
1/2 cup pineapple chunks
1/3 cup sliced banana
1/2 cup honeydew melon chunks
1/2 cup pineapple juice
1 tablespoon honey
3/4 teaspoon lemon juice
1 cup cran-grape juice
banana slices

Blend first eight ingredients until smooth. Serve immediately with banana slice garnishing side of glass. Makes 2 servings.

Peachy Blend

2 cups milk
2 cups ice
1 banana, sliced
2 14-ounce cans peaches
1 teaspoon sugar
maraschino cherries

Combine first five ingredients in blender and blend until smooth. Serve immediately in frosty mug. Garnish with maraschino cherry. Makes 2 servings.

It's a Wonderful Lime

1 ½ cups sugar
4 cups boiling water
1 6-ounce can frozen limeade, slightly thawed
ice cubes
1 2-liter bottle 7 UP®
fresh lime slices

Combine sugar and water. Stir until sugar is dissolved. Add limeade and freeze mixture overnight. Allow to thaw until slushy. Fill glass about ⅓ full with limeade slush and add ice cubes. Fill glass with 7 UP®. Garnish with fresh lime slice. Makes 10 servings.

Summer 7 UP® Fruit Cooler

    4 bananas
    2 cups crushed pineapple with juice
    2 cups orange juice
    ¾ cup sugar
    2 tablespoons lemon juice
    pinch of salt
    1 2-liter bottle 7 UP®

Blend all ingredients except 7 UP®. Pour mixture into freezer bags and freeze until slushy. To serve, fill glasses about ⅓ full with fruit juice slush. Fill glasses with 7 UP®. Makes 6–8 servings.

Citrus Breeze

    1 cup orange juice
    ½ cup crushed pineapple
    1 teaspoon lemon juice
    ½ cup Canada Dry® Ginger Ale
    1 cup ice
    orange slices

Blend first five ingredients in blender until smooth and ice is crushed. Garnish with orange slices. Serve immediately. Makes 2 servings.

Pineapple Ice

1 quart pineapple sherbet
1 cup Canada Dry® Club Soda
maraschino cherries

Blend sherbet and Canada Dry® Club Soda. Serve in parfait glasses and garnish each with a maraschino cherry. Makes 4–6 servings.

Apple Strawberry Surprise

1 cup frozen strawberries, thawed
2 ½ cups MOTT'S® apple juice
½ teaspoon sugar
1 2-liter bottle Canada Dry® Ginger Ale, chilled
fresh strawberries

Blend berries, MOTT'S® apple juice, and sugar until smooth. Pour into glasses, filling each glass half full. Fill the remainder of each glass with chilled Canada Dry® Ginger Ale. Garnish with fresh strawberry. Makes 4 servings.

Strawberry 7 UP® Cooler

1 ½ cups frozen strawberries
juice of ½ lemon
3 cups 7 UP®
2 cups crushed ice
lemon slices

Blend first four ingredients on high in blender until ice is crushed. Serve immediately in frosty mugs. Garnish with fresh lemon slice. Makes 4 servings.

Peach Lovers' Delight

½ cup peach nectar
1 cup fresh peaches, peeled and cut
dash grenadine
½ cup Canada Dry® Sparkling Water
1 teaspoon sugar
2 cups crushed ice
maraschino cherries

Blend first six ingredients until well mixed. Serve in frosted mugs with a maraschino cherry. Makes 2 servings.

Pretty in Pink

  2 cups fresh strawberries
  2 cups watermelon, cut in chunks and seeded
  ½ cup sugar
  juice from ½ lemon
  1 cup ice
  fresh strawberries

Combine first four ingredients in blender. Blend until mixed. Gradually add ice, blending until smooth. Garnish with fresh strawberry. Makes 2 servings.

Very Strawberry Freeze

  2 cups fresh strawberries
  1 cup water
  1 tablespoon sugar
  4 cups ice
  4 large marshmallows
  ¾ cup strawberry nectar
  fresh strawberries

Blend first six ingredients until smooth. Garnish with fresh strawberry. Makes 2 servings.

Summer Slush

1 46-ounce can pineapple juice
4 ½ cups Canada Dry® Ginger Ale
1 12-ounce can strawberry nectar
fresh strawberries

Combine first three ingredients and stir until thoroughly mixed. Place in freezer for about four hours, stirring every 30–40 minutes. When slushy, spoon into parfait glasses, garnish with fresh strawberry and serve. Makes 12 servings.

Icy Chocolate Milk

1 ½ cups milk
4 tablespoons chocolate syrup
½ teaspoon vanilla
1 ½ cups crushed ice
chocolate shavings

Combine first four ingredients in blender and blend until slushy. Serve in frosty mug and sprinkle with chocolate shavings. Makes 2 servings.

Pineapple Freeze

3 cups crushed ice
2 cups pineapple juice
1 cup fresh pineapple
1 cup 7 UP®
4 tablespoons sugar
maraschino cherries

Combine first five ingredients in blender. Blend until ice is crushed and ingredients are mixed well. Serve immediately in wine glasses. Garnish with maraschino cherries. Makes 2 servings.

Peach-Strawberry Slush

½ cup Canada Dry® Club Soda
3 cups crushed ice
½ cup strawberry nectar
½ cup peach nectar
fresh strawberries

Blend first four ingredients until slushy. Pour into parfait glasses and garnish with fresh strawberries. Serve immediately. Makes 2 servings.

Strawberry Lemonade Icy

    1 ½ cups strawberries
    1 6-ounce can frozen lemonade concentrate,
        thawed
    1 cup ice
    1 ½ cups Canada Dry® Ginger Ale
    lemon slices

Place first four ingredients in blender and blend until smooth. Pour in tall glasses and garnish with fresh lemon slices. Makes 2 servings.

Raspberry-Lime Slush

    1 ½ cups raspberries
    1 6-ounce can frozen limeade concentrate, thawed
    2 tablespoons sugar
    2 cups crushed ice
    1 ½ cups Canada Dry® Ginger Ale
    lime slices

Place first five ingredients in blender and blend until smooth and frothy. Pour into tall glasses and garnish with fresh lime slices. Make 3–4 servings.

Peach Slush

6 peaches, peeled, pitted, and sliced
1 ½ cups apricot nectar
½ cup sugar
½ teaspoon freshly grated lemon peel
½ teaspoon lemon juice
maraschino cherries

Combine first five ingredients in blender and puree. Pour into container. Cover and freeze overnight. Break frozen mixture and put in blender again. Blend until slushy. Serve in parfait glasses and garnish with maraschino cherry. Makes 2 servings.

Fruit Slush

2 oranges
2 lemons
1 banana, sliced
1 cup sugar (more if desired)
1 ½ cups Canada Dry® Ginger Ale
½ cup crushed pineapple
fresh cherries

Squeeze juice from oranges and lemons. Combine juice and pour into blender. Add next four ingredients to blender and blend until smooth. Pour in parfait glasses and garnish with fresh cherry. Makes 2 servings.

Orange Julia

1 6-ounce can frozen orange juice concentrate,
        thawed
1 ½ cups milk
½ cup water
1 teaspoon vanilla
½ cup sugar
1 tray ice cubes
orange slices
mint sprigs

Blend first six ingredients until smooth. Serve in parfait glasses and garnish with a fresh orange slice and mint sprigs. Makes 3–4 servings.

Kokomo Ice Blend

1 cup fruit punch
1 6-ounce can frozen limeade concentrate, thawed
½ cup cream of coconut
½ tablespoon rum flavoring
1 cup water
ice
lime slices

Combine first six ingredients in blender and blend until mixed well. Serve immediately in small glasses with fresh lime slices. Makes 2 servings.

Peach Moonbeam

½ blender of crushed ice
4 fresh peaches, peeled and pitted
juice of ½ lemon
2 tablespoons sugar
maraschino cherries

Combine first four ingredients in blender and blend until ice is crushed. Serve in parfait glasses and garnish with a maraschino cherry. Makes 2 servings.

Vanilla Ice Ice Baby

3 scoops vanilla ice cream
½ cup milk
3 cups crushed ice
½ teaspoon vanilla extract

Blend all ingredients until smooth. Serve when slushy. Makes 2 servings.

Tropical Citrus Slush

2 oranges
2 lemons
1 cup sugar
2 cups crushed pineapple with juice
pineapple juice
2 cups Canada Dry® Ginger Ale
3 bananas, mashed

Squeeze juice from oranges and lemons. Grate rinds of 1 orange and 1 lemon and set aside. Combine juices with sugar, crushed pineapple, Canada Dry® Ginger Ale, bananas, and orange and lemon rinds. Pour into container and freeze. Thaw 20–30 minutes before serving. Makes 4–6 servings.

Plum Slush

8 plums, peeled and pitted
1 cup pineapple juice
¼ cup sugar
¼ teaspoon lime juice
¼ teaspoon grated lime peel
pineapple chunks

Combine first five ingredients in blender and puree. Pour into container and freeze overnight. When ready to serve, break frozen mixture and return to blender. Blend until slushy. Serve in tall glasses with fresh pineapple chunks on toothpicks. Makes 2 servings.

CHAPTER

2

Ice Cream Shakes

Another great way to cool off in the heat of the summer is with your favorite ice cream or yogurt shake. These creamy treats can always be made low fat or no fat by substituting fat-free yogurt for ice cream. Of course, feel free to splurge with the real thing. You and your guests deserve it!

Creamy Fruit Blend

1 scoop vanilla ice cream
½ banana, sliced
1 cup sugar
1 tablespoon vanilla
1 12-ounce can orange juice concentrate, thawed
1 6-ounce can limeade concentrate, thawed
ice
1 2-liter bottle 7 UP®
lime slices

Blend ice cream and banana until smooth. Pour into large pitcher and add next four ingredients. Let stand about 1–2 hours. Pour juice mixture into glasses (fill about half full) over ice. Fill glasses with 7 UP®. Garnish with fresh lime slices. Makes 10 servings.

The Breakfast Club Shake

1 ½ cups grapefruit juice
1 cup freshly squeezed orange juice
1 scoop orange sherbet
1 cup Canada Dry® Club Soda
lime slices

Mix juices with orange sherbet and pour into chilled glasses. Add Canada Dry® Club Soda. Garnish with fresh lime slices. Makes 2 servings.

Friends in Low Places

¾ cup chocolate syrup
whipped cream
1 quart vanilla ice cream
2 cups milk
½ teaspoon cinnamon
¼ cup chocolate shavings

Spoon 2 tablespoons chocolate syrup into chilled parfait glasses. Scoop small spoonful of whipped cream on top of syrup. Combine ice cream, milk, and cinnamon in blender. Pour mixture over whipped cream in glasses. Pour one additional spoonful of chocolate syrup over the top of ice cream mixture. Top with whipped cream and chocolate shavings. Makes 4 servings.

Peaches and Cream

6 fresh peaches, pitted, peeled, and sliced
1 cup milk
1 tablespoon lemon juice
4 scoops vanilla ice cream
2 tablespoons powdered sugar
whipped cream
fresh cherries

Combine first five ingredients in blender. Blend until smooth. Serve immediately in frosty mugs. Garnish with whipped cream and fresh cherry. Makes 4 servings.

Uptown Swirl

    2 scoops strawberry ice cream
    2 cups Canada Dry® Ginger Ale
    1 cup peach nectar
    ½ cup crushed ice
    fresh strawberries

Mix first four ingredients in blender until smooth. Pour into frosted mug and garnish with fresh whole strawberry. Makes 2 servings.

Tropical Milk Shake

    4 bananas, sliced
    ⅔ cup orange juice
    4 scoops pineapple sherbet
    3 tablespoons honey
    pinch of salt
    2 cups cold milk
    whipped cream
    shredded coconut

Combine first six ingredients in blender and blend until smooth. Pour in specialty glasses. Top with whipped cream and coconut. Makes 4 servings.

Fruity Yogurt Shake

1 ½ cups mango nectar
1 cup fresh pineapple
1 teaspoon sugar
2 large scoops vanilla ice cream
1 banana, sliced
2 tablespoons honey
fresh cherries

Blend first six ingredients together until smooth. Serve in specialty glasses with fresh cherry for garnish. Makes 2 servings.

Maple-Coffee Float

4 cups strong hot coffee
1 teaspoon ground cinnamon
¾ cup maple syrup
3 scoops vanilla ice cream
ground cinnamon

Combine coffee and cinnamon. Add syrup and chill. Place 1 scoop of ice cream in each of 3 glasses. Stir coffee mixture well and pour about ¾ cup of mixture over ice cream. Sprinkle with cinnamon. Makes 3 servings.

Apple Pie Shake

    2 scoops vanilla ice cream
    1 cup MOTT'S® apple juice
    ½ cup crushed ice
    2 teaspoons cinnamon
    whipped cream
    cinnamon sprinkles

Blend first four ingredients until smooth. Serve in frosty cold mugs. Top with whipped cream and cinnamon sprinkles. Makes 2 servings.

Lime Sorbet Freeze

    3 scoops lime sherbet
    2 cups 7 UP®
    2 cups crushed ice
    lime slices

Combine sherbet, 7 UP®, and ice in blender. Mix until ice is crushed. Pour into parfait glasses and serve. Garnish with fresh lime slice. Makes 2 servings.

Strawberry-Chocolate Shake

4 scoops vanilla ice cream
1 cup fresh strawberries
½ cup strawberry nectar
4 tablespoons chocolate syrup
2 teaspoons sugar
fresh strawberries

Blend first five ingredients together until smooth and creamy. Serve in parfait glasses and garnish with fresh strawberries. Makes 2 servings.

Dessert Drink

⅛ cup strong coffee
4 tablespoons chocolate syrup
¾ cup Canada Dry® Club Soda
2 large scoops vanilla ice cream
whipped cream
chocolate shavings

Blend first four ingredients until well mixed and pour into mugs. Garnish with whipped cream and chocolate shavings. Makes 2 servings.

Grasshopper Dessert Drink

1 ¼ cups coffee, cooled
2 scoops chocolate ice cream
2 teaspoons brown sugar
1 teaspoon mint flavoring
whipped cream
brown sugar

Blend first four ingredients. Pour into two tall glasses. Serve with a dollop of whipped cream and sprinkle with brown sugar. Makes 2 servings.

Bananarama Shake

½ cup frozen orange juice concentrate, thawed
1 banana, sliced
3 scoops vanilla ice cream
½ cup cold milk

Combine orange juice, banana, and ice cream in blender. Mix until well blended. Slowly add milk and blend until smooth. Pour into frosted mugs. Makes 2 servings.

Her Name Is Rio

1 cup orange juice
½ cup pineapple juice
2 large scoops strawberry sherbet
½ cup fresh strawberries, halved and topped
2 teaspoons sugar
whole strawberries

Combine first five ingredients in blender and mix until smooth. Serve in frosted parfait glass with whole strawberry on top. Serves 2.

Raisin Arizona Shake

1 pint vanilla ice cream
1 cup milk
¼ cup raisins
1 teaspoon ground cinnamon
1 teaspoon vanilla extract
cinnamon sprinkles

Combine first five ingredients in blender. Mix until smooth. Sprinkle with cinnamon and serve immediately. Makes 2–4 servings

Mom's Old-Fashioned Chocolate Shake

    4 scoops vanilla ice cream
    4 tablespoons chocolate syrup
    1 cup crushed ice
    ½ teaspoon vanilla
    2 teaspoons sugar
    ½ cup milk
    whipped cream
    chopped nuts
    chocolate shavings

Blend first six ingredients until smooth and creamy. Serve in frosty mugs and top with whipped cream, chopped nuts, and chocolate shavings. Makes 2 large servings.

Sherbet Shake

    1 cup MOTT'S® apple juice
    2 large scoops orange sherbet
    1 cup crushed ice
    orange slices

Combine first three ingredients in blender and mix well. Serve in frosty mugs garnished with fresh orange slices. Makes 2 servings.

Raspberry-Plum Shake

3–4 plums, peeled and pitted
½ cup fresh raspberries
3 teaspoons sugar
1 cup crushed ice
2 large scoops vanilla ice cream
fresh raspberries

Blend plums, raspberries, sugar, and ice in blender. Add ice cream and mix until thoroughly blended. Pour into tall glasses and garnish with fresh raspberries. Makes 2 servings.

Chocolate Lover's Dream

2 scoops chocolate ice cream
2 tablespoons chocolate syrup
¼ cup milk
¼ cup crushed ice
chocolate shavings
whipped cream

Combine first four ingredients in blender and mix until thoroughly blended. Pour into frosted mugs. Top with whipped cream and chocolate shavings. Serves 2.

A Taste of the Tropics

2 scoops orange sherbet
2 cups fresh pineapple chunks with juice
2 teaspoons sugar
1 cup crushed ice
fresh pineapple chunks

Blend first four ingredients until smooth. Serve in parfait glasses. Garnish with fresh pineapple chunks. Makes 2 servings.

Orange Freeze

1 pint orange sherbet
2 cups orange juice
2 cups crushed ice
orange slices

Combine sherbet, juice, and ice in blender. Blend until thick and frosty. Serve in chilled parfait glasses. Garnish with orange slices. Makes 3–4 servings.

Coconutty Milk Shake

    4 scoops vanilla ice cream
    2 teaspoons cream of coconut
    4 tablespoons chocolate
    ½ cup milk
    grated coconut

Combine first four ingredients in blender and mix until thick and creamy (only about 10 seconds). Serve in frosty mugs or specialty glasses. Garnish with grated coconut. Makes 3–4 servings.

Fruity Blend

    1 cup cranberry juice
    1 orange, peeled and sliced
    1 teaspoon sugar
    1 cup vanilla ice cream
    maraschino cherries

Combine cranberry juice, orange, and sugar in blender. Blend on high speed until smooth. Add ice cream and blend again, just until well mixed. Serve immediately with maraschino cherry for garnish. Makes 1 serving.

Happy Apple Freeze

1 apple, chopped
½ cup MOTT'S® apple juice
3 scoops vanilla ice cream
1 tablespoon cinnamon
1 tablespoon sugar
2 cinnamon sticks

Blend apple and MOTT'S® apple juice until mixed well. Add ice cream, cinnamon, and sugar and blend again briefly. Serve in frosted mug with cinnamon stick. Makes 2 servings.

Blueberry Thrill

2 scoops vanilla ice cream
1 6-ounce carton blueberry yogurt
2 cups fresh blueberries
2 teaspoons sugar
fresh blueberries

Blend first four ingredients until smooth. Serve in mug with fresh blueberries on top. Makes 2 servings.

Moon River Blend

2 cups milk
1 pint vanilla ice cream
½ cup frozen orange juice concentrate, slightly
    thawed
orange slices

Combine milk, ice cream, and orange juice in blender.
Blend until smooth. Pour into chilled parfait glasses and
garnish with orange slice. Makes 4 servings.

Fresh 'n Fruity Shake

2 scoops lime sherbet
¼ cup crushed pineapple
¼ cup fresh strawberries
1 teaspoon sugar
lime slices

Combine first four ingredients in blender and mix until
smooth. Garnish with fresh lime slice. Makes 2 servings.

Apricot Shake

1 ½ cups apricot nectar
¼ cup milk
2 teaspoons lemon juice
1 pint vanilla ice cream
fresh cherries

Blend first four ingredients until smooth. Garnish with
fresh cherry. Makes 4 servings.

Chocolate Mint Delight

> 4 large scoops of vanilla ice cream
> ¼ cup chocolate syrup
> 2 teaspoons mint flavoring
> peppermint sticks

Blend first three ingredients until consistency of thick milk shake. Serve in parfait glasses. Garnish with a peppermint stick. Makes 4 servings.

Banana Shake

> 2 scoops vanilla ice cream
> ½ cup packed brown sugar
> ½ teaspoon vanilla
> ½ cup crushed ice
> 2 bananas, sliced
> brown sugar

Combine first five ingredients in blender and blend until smooth. Serve in tall glasses and sprinkle with brown sugar. Makes 2 servings.

Dr Pepper® Malt

3 scoops chocolate ice cream
1 6-ounce bottle Dr Pepper®
2 teaspoons malted milk
maraschino cherries

Place ice cream and Dr Pepper® in blender. Add malted milk. Blend until thoroughly mixed. Garnish with maraschino cherry. Makes 2 servings.

My Little Butterscotch

2 scoops vanilla ice cream
½ cup ice
½ banana, sliced
2 tablespoons butterscotch topping
chopped nuts

Blend first four ingredients until smooth. Pour in frosty mugs and sprinkle with chopped nuts. Makes 2 servings.

Strawberry Shake

½ banana, sliced
1 cup fresh strawberries, halved
2 teaspoons sugar
2 large scoops strawberry ice cream
½ cup strawberry nectar
fresh strawberries

Combine banana, strawberries, and sugar in blender and blend until thoroughly mixed. Add ice cream and nectar. Blend until smooth. Serve immediately and garnish with fresh strawberry. Makes 2 servings.

Strawberry-Lime Freeze

2 scoops lime sherbet
2 cups fresh strawberries, halved and topped
2 tablespoons sugar
1 cup 7 UP®
fresh strawberries

Combine first four ingredients in blender and mix. Serve in parfait glasses and garnish with a fresh strawberry. Makes 2 servings.

Fresh Pineapple Shake

1 cup pineapple juice
1 cup fresh pineapple chunks
2 teaspoons sugar
1 cup crushed ice
2 scoops vanilla ice cream
maraschino cherries

Combine first four ingredients in blender. Blend until ice is crushed. Add ice cream and blend briefly until mixed. Serve immediately with maraschino cherries in frosted mugs. Makes 2 servings.

CHAPTER

3

Ice Cream Floats

Perhaps the easiest ice cream treat to create is the old-fashioned ice cream float. These days, floats are anything but old-fashioned. Try your hand at a delicious new fruity blend or rich chocolate mix. Be creative!

Dr Pepper® Float

> 1 pint vanilla ice cream
> 2 cups Dr Pepper®, chilled
> maraschino cherries

Place one large scoop of ice cream in each of two large glasses. Slowly fill with chilled Dr Pepper®. Gently place another ice cream scoop on top. Garnish each with a maraschino cherry. Makes 2 servings.

Tropical Heat Wave Float

> 2 scoops pineapple sherbet
> 1 cup Canada Dry® Ginger Ale
> 1 cup fruit punch
> pineapple chunk
> maraschino cherries

Place 1 scoop sherbet into each parfait glass. Fill each glass with ½ cup Canada Dry® Ginger Ale and ½ cup fruit punch. Garnish with a pineapple chunk and maraschino cherry. Makes 2 servings.

A&W® Root Beer Float

> 1 pint vanilla ice cream
> 2 cups A&W® Root Beer
> maraschino cherries

In each of two large glasses, place one large scoop of ice cream. Slowly pour A&W® Root Beer to fill glass. Serve with straw and spoon and a maraschino cherry on top. Makes 2 servings.

Peppermint Float

1 quart peppermint ice cream
4 tablespoons finely crushed peppermint candy
4 cups milk
½ pint whipped cream

Combine 1 pint peppermint ice cream and 2 tablespoons crushed candies in blender. Gradually blend in milk and blend until smooth. Pour into chilled glasses over a scoop of peppermint ice cream. Scoop a spoonful of whipped cream on top of mixture and garnish with remaining peppermint candies. Makes 4 servings.

Pink Lady Float

1 6-ounce can frozen fruit punch concentrate,
    thawed
1 quart milk
1 pint raspberry sherbet
strawberries
mint sprigs

Combine fruit punch and milk in blender. Pour into tall chilled glasses and top with scoops of sherbet. Garnish with fresh strawberries and mint sprigs. Makes 6–8 servings.

Tropicale Float

    2 cups pineapple juice
    4 scoops pineapple sherbet
    1 small can crushed pineapple
    2 cups Canada Dry® Ginger Ale
    maraschino cherries

Fill 4 glasses, each half-way to the top with juice. Put 1 scoop of sherbet in each glass. Add a spoonful of crushed pineapple to each glass and mix with sherbet. Pour Canada Dry® Ginger Ale in each glass until full and gently stir. Add a maraschino cherry for garnish. Makes 4 servings.

Strawberry Fields Forever Float

    2 scoops strawberry ice cream
    1 cup fresh strawberries, topped and quartered
    1 ½ cups Canada Dry® Ginger Ale
    fresh strawberries

Place one scoop of ice cream in each of two glasses. Spoon ½ cup of berries in each glass. Fill with Canada Dry® Ginger Ale and stir gently. Garnish with fresh strawberry. Makes 2 servings.

Pineapple-Strawberry Float

    2 scoops strawberry ice cream
    1 cup fresh strawberries, topped and quartered
    2 tablespoons fresh crushed pineapple
    1½ cup pinapple juice
    ½ cup Canada Dry® Ginger Ale
    pineapple chunks
    whole strawberries

Scoop ice cream in parfait glasses. Add a few strawberries and 1 tablespoon pineapple. Fill each glass with ¾ cup pinapple juice and ¼ cup Canada Dry® Ginger Ale. Garnish each glass with pineapple chunk and a whole strawberry on toothpick. Makes 2 servings.

Chocolate Chip Float

4 scoops chocolate chip ice cream
2 cups Dr Pepper®
fresh cherries

Place 1 scoop of ice cream in each of two tall parfait glasses. Add about 1 cup Dr Pepper® to each. Gently stir ice cream. Add second scoop of ice cream to each glass and top with remaining Dr Pepper®. Garnish with fresh cherry. Makes 2 servings.

Cherry Float

2 scoops vanilla ice cream
2 cups Canada Dry® Ginger Ale
½ maraschino cherry juice
maraschino cherries

Place one scoop of ice cream into each of two tall chilled glasses. Pour 1 cup Canada Dry® Ginger Ale and cup maraschino cherry juice into glasses and garnish with a cherry. Makes 2 servings.

Saturday Night Fever Float

2 cups milk
2 cups Dr Pepper®
1 tablespoon chocolate syrup
2 scoops vanilla ice cream
maraschino cherries

Blend milk, Dr Pepper®, and chocolate syrup in blender until well mixed. Fill parfait glasses about ½ full with Dr Pepper® mixture and top with a scoop of ice cream. Fill glasses with remaining Dr Pepper® mixture. Garnish with a maraschino cherry. Makes 2 servings.

Pineapple Soda Float

2 cups Canada Dry® Ginger Ale
1 cup cranberry juice
1 cup pineapple juice
¼ cup lemon juice
1 pint pineapple sherbet
lime slices

Combine Canada Dry® Ginger Ale and juices in blender and mix well. Pour in tall glasses and gently top with one scoop of pineapple sherbet. Garnish with fresh lime slice. Makes 4 servings.

Chocolate Soda

4 large scoops of vanilla ice cream
4–6 tablespoons chocolate syrup
1 2-liter bottle Canada Dry® Sparkling Water

Mix one scoop of ice cream with chocolate syrup in bottom of glass. Fill glass ¾ full with Canada Dry® Sparkling Water. Carefully add final scoop of ice cream. Serve with straw and spoon. Makes 2 servings.

Texas Longhorn Slush

    1 cup Sunkist® Orange Soda
    2 cups 7 UP®
    1 6-ounce can frozen orange juice
    1 can cold water
    1 pint vanilla ice cream
    orange slices

Mix first four ingredients. Freeze, stirring every 40 minutes until it reaches slushy consistency. When ready to serve, place 1 scoop vanilla ice cream in each glass and fill glasses with slushy orange mixture. Garnish with fresh orange slice. Makes 6 servings.

CHAPTER

4

Heart Warmers

Nothing comforts the heart on a cold winter day like a warm cup of cocoa or spiced cider. Try a couple of these new treats along with some old cozy favorites. Surprise your guests with a fun new twist. You never know—some may like it hot!

Some Like It Hot

3 cups Dr Pepper®
3 cups cranberry juice
lemon slices

Combine first two ingredients in large pot on stove and heat to boiling. Reduce heat and simmer for about 15–20 minutes. Serve hot in mugs and garnish with lemon slice. Makes 6 servings.

Coconut Coffee

1 cup strong coffee
1 tablespoon coconut cream
¼ teaspoon rum flavoring
whipped cream
grated coconut

Make coffee as instructed. Pour coffee in mug. Add coconut cream and rum flavoring. Stir well. Top with whipped cream and grated coconut. Makes 1 serving.

Rum Coffee

4 cups strong black coffee
1 tablespoon sugar
¼ cup milk
1 teaspoon rum flavoring

Prepare coffee. Add sugar while coffee is still hot. Stir. Add milk and rum. Beat with electric mixer on low. Before serving, bring to a boil and serve hot. Makes 4 servings.

Cocoa Coffee

¼ cup instant coffee
⅓ cup sugar
¼ cup powdered nondairy coffee
    creamer
2 tablespoons powdered cocoa
1 cup boiling water
whipped cream
chocolate sprinkles

Mix first four ingredients thoroughly. Place in container. To serve, combine 1 teaspoon of coffee mix with ¾ cup boiling water. Stir well. Serve with whipped cream and chocolate sprinkles. Makes 1 serving.

Almond Coffee

¾ cup coffee
½ teaspoon almond extract
whipped cream

Mix coffee and almond extract in mug. Top with whipped cream. Serve hot. Makes 1 serving.

Peanut Butter Coffee

2 cups coffee
2 cups milk
2 tablespoons sugar
2 tablespoons creamy peanut butter
½ teaspoon vanilla

Combine all ingredients in a large saucepan. Heat to boiling, then simmer 10–15 minutes, stirring occasionally. Serve hot. Makes 4 servings.

Cappuccino

1 cinnamon stick
3–4 whole cloves
⅛ cup instant coffee
⅛ cup sugar
1 ½ cups boiling water
¾ cup half & half, warmed
½ cup whipped cream
nutmeg

Place cinnamon stick and cloves in small pot. Add coffee and sugar. Pour in boiling water to dissolve. Cover and steep about 5–10 minutes. Remove cinnamon stick and cloves. Add half & half. Serve in warm mugs and top with whipped cream. Sprinkle with nutmeg. Makes 4 servings.

Cafe Au Lait

1 cup strong black coffee
1 cup hot milk
½ teaspoon sugar

Brew strong black coffee. Pour coffee and milk simultaneously into cup. Stir in sugar until dissolved. Makes 2 servings.

Tea Thyme

    3 quarts water
    2 tea bags
    juice of 2 lemons
    ½ gallon apple juice
    1 cup orange juice
    1 cup sugar
    3 cinnamon sticks
    1 teaspoon whole cloves
    dash of thyme
    16 cinnamon sticks

Bring water to boil. Add tea bags and steep for 5–10 minutes. Reduce to medium heat and add next seven ingredients. Stir. Before serving, remove cloves and cinnamon sticks with slotted spoon. Serve hot in mugs with cinnamon sticks to garnish. Makes 16 servings.

Hot Cranberry Tea

    1 pound fresh cranberries
    2 quarts water
    2 cups water
    1 ½ cups sugar
    3 tablespoons lemon juice
    2 cups cinnamon sticks
    2 cups orange juice

Cook cranberries in 2 quarts of water on high heat until berries pop. Let stand about 10 minutes. Strain cranberries, separating berries from skins. Combine berries, 2 cups water, sugar, lemon juice, and cinnamon sticks in pot and bring to a boil. Add orange juice and stir. Strain tea and serve immediately. Makes 10 servings.

Spiced Tea Mix

1 ¼ cups sugar
1 cup instant orange-flavored drink mix
1 cup instant tea
1 ½ cups instant lemonade
1 teaspoon nutmeg
1 teaspoon ground cloves
1 teaspoon cinnamon

Mix all above ingredients and store in tightly closed container. To serve, place 2 heaping teaspoons mix in a mug and fill with hot water. Mix makes about 24 servings.

Hot Almond Tea

3 tea bags
6 cups water
⅔ cup fresh lemon juice
1 cup sugar
2 teaspoons almond extract
1 teaspoon vanilla

Steep tea bags in 2 cups boiling water for 10 minutes. Add lemon juice, sugar, flavorings, and remaining 4 cups water. Serve hot. Makes 6–8 servings.

Hot Buttered "Rum" Mix

    1 ½ cups brown sugar
    ½ cup butter
    ½ tablespoon ground cinnamon
    1 teaspoon allspice
    ¼ teaspoon ground cloves
    ¼ teaspoon nutmeg
    rum flavoring
    hot water
    cinnamon sticks

Combine first 6 ingredients in large mixing bowl. Beat with electric mixer until fluffy. Refrigerate in covered container. To serve, place 1 heaping tablespoon of mix and ½ teaspoon rum flavoring in mug. Add hot water and stir. Garnish with cinnamon stick. Mix makes about 25 servings.

Rumpelstiltzkin

3 cups brown sugar

3 cups sugar

2 sticks of butter, softened

1 quart vanilla ice cream, softened

1 teaspoon cinnamon

1 teaspoon nutmeg

rum flavoring

1 cup boiling water

cinnamon sticks (optional)

Cream sugars and butter together. Add ice cream and spices and mix well. To serve, put 1 heaping tablespoon in cup with 1 teaspoon rum flavoring. Add 1 cup boiling water. Garnish with cinnamon stick if desired. Mix makes about 20 servings.

Spicy Fruit Cider

½ cup brown sugar
2 ½ cups pineapple juice
2 cups cranberry juice
1 ½ cups water
1 tablespoon whole cloves
2 tablespoons cinnamon
1 tea bag
cinnamon sticks

Mix brown sugar, pineapple juice, cranberry juice, and water in large pot. Add cloves, ground cinnamon, and tea bag. Bring to a boil, then turn heat down to low. Simmer for about 15 minutes. Before serving, remove cloves with a slotted spoon. Serve in mugs and garnish with cinnamon sticks. Makes about 6 servings.

Miss Betty's Hot Apricot Cider

3 cups apricot nectar
2 cups orange juice
2 tablespoons lime juice
1 cup water
¼ cup brown sugar
3–4 cinnamon sticks
½ teaspoon whole cloves
cinnamon sticks

In large saucepan, combine nectar, juices, water, and sugar. Tie cinnamon and cloves in cheesecloth bag. Heat to boiling. Reduce heat and simmer about 15 minutes. Discard spice bag. Serve in mugs or hot punch cups with cinnamon sticks to garnish. Makes about 6 servings.

Susan's Spiced Cider

1 quart MOTT'S® apple juice
1 cup orange juice
½ cup lemon juice
1 ½ cups pineapple juice
1–2 sticks cinnamon
½ teaspoon whole cloves
⅛ cup sugar
orange slices

Combine first seven ingredients in large pot and simmer for about 1 hour. Serve hot in mugs. Garnish with orange slices. Makes about 6 servings.

Grape Balls of Fire

    4 cups grape juice
    2 cups MOTT'S® apple juice
    2 cups Canada Dry® Ginger Ale
    lemon slices

Combine first three ingredients in pot and simmer for 15–20 minutes. Serve hot in mugs. Garnish mugs with lemon slices. Makes 6–8 servings.

Granny's Apple Cider

    1 ½ quarts MOTT'S® apple juice
    ⅓ cup cinnamon candies
    1 tablespoon whole cloves
    cinnamon sticks

Pour MOTT'S® apple juice in percolator. Place cinnamon candies and cloves in basket and perk. (Without a percolator, combine all ingredients in large pot on stove. Warm over medium heat and simmer for about 15–20 minutes. Remove cloves with a slotted spoon before serving.) Serve hot in mugs with cinnamon sticks to garnish. Makes 6–8 servings.

Hot and Spicy Orange Cider

¼ cup sugar
1 cup water
½ teaspoon ground cinnamon
6 whole cloves
1 quart orange juice
1 pint MOTT'S® apple juice
cinnamon sticks

Combine sugar, water, ground cinnamon, and cloves in saucepan. Simmer about 10 minutes. Remove cloves with slotted spoon. Add orange juice and MOTT'S® apple juice, stirring well. Serve hot in mugs. Garnish with cinnamon stick. Makes 6–8 servings.

Hot Toddy

1 ½ cups cranberry juice
2 small slices of orange peel
splash of MOTT'S® apple juice
2 teaspoons ground cinnamon
cinnamon sticks

In a saucepan, heat cranberry juice with orange peel, just to boiling. Remove orange peel and pour cranberry juice into mugs. Stir in splash of MOTT'S® apple juice and garnish with cinnamon sprinkles. Serve with cinnamon sticks to stir. Makes 2 servings.

Cranberry Caper

    1 quart cranberry juice
    1 tablespoon ground cinnamon
    1 slice of orange peel
    1 tablespoon honey
    3 tea bags
    cinnamon sticks

In a large saucepan, heat cranberry juice, cinnamon, orange peel, and honey, just to boiling. Remove from heat. Add tea bags. Cover and let stand about 5–10 minutes. Remove tea bags and orange peel. Pour into mugs and serve hot with cinnamon sticks as stirs. Makes 4–6 servings.

Easy Cranapple Cider

    4 cups MOTT'S® apple juice
    4 cups cranberry juice
    2 teaspoons cinnamon
    2 teaspoons sugar
    cinnamon sticks

Combine first four ingredients in a pot and heat, stirring occasionally. Simmer about 20–25 minutes. Serve warm in mugs with cinnamon stick to garnish. Makes about 8 servings.

Love Me Tender Cider

4 cups cranberry juice
4 cups pineapple juice
2 cups water
½ cup brown sugar
2 tablespoons cinnamon
2 teaspoons whole cloves

Heat juices, water, and brown sugar in saucepan. Add cinnamon and cloves. Bring to a boil. Reduce heat and simmer. Remove cloves with slotted spoon and serve hot. Makes 10 servings.

Hot Peanut Butter Chocolate

⅓ cup cocoa
½ cup sugar
¼ teaspoon cinnamon
½ cup creamy peanut butter
4 cups milk
whipped cream
chopped peanuts

Combine cocoa, sugar, and cinnamon in a saucepan. Add peanut butter and milk, and heat on medium heat about 20 minutes, stirring frequently. Serve hot. Top with whipped cream and chopped peanuts. Makes 4 servings.

Coconutty Hot Cocoa

 3 tablespoons hot cocoa mix
 1 teaspoon cream of coconut
 ¾ cup hot water
 whipped cream
 maraschino cherry

Combine cocoa mix and cream of coconut in mug. Slowly stir in hot water. Top with whipped cream and cherry. Makes 1 serving.

Almond Hot Chocolate

 3 tablespoons instant hot cocoa mix
 ½ teaspoon almond extract
 1 cup boiling water
 whipped cream
 ground cinnamon

Combine instant cocoa and almond extract in mug. Slowly add boiling water while stirring. Top with whipped cream and cinnamon. Makes 1 serving.

Hot Cinnamon Chocolate

3 heaping tablespoons instant hot cocoa mix
½ tablespoon cinnamon
2 tablespoons milk
½ teaspoon sugar
¼ teaspoon honey
¾ cup boiling water
whipped cream
cinnamon sprinkles

Combine first five ingredients in mug. Add boiling water and stir. Garnish with whipped cream and cinnamon sprinkles. Makes 1 serving.

Hot Mint Chocolate

3 tablespoons hot cocoa mix
2 teaspoons peppermint flavoring
¾ cup hot water
candy cane

Combine hot cocoa mix and 1 teaspoon peppermint flavoring in mug. Fill mug with hot water, stirring well. Garnish with candy cane. Makes 1 serving.

Decadent Hot Chocolate

2 cups milk
4 tablespoons chocolate syrup
2 teaspoons almond flavoring
marshmallow cream
dash of cinnamon

Combine milk, chocolate syrup, and almond flavoring in saucepan. Heat and simmer about 10 minutes. Pour into mugs. Top with marshmallow cream and cinnamon. Makes 2 servings.

CHAPTER

5

Cold Drinks

Everyone knows that a refreshing glass of lemonade or iced tea hits the spot in the summertime. Now you can add these new variations to your list of favorite refreshers. Whether you're enjoying a porch swing with an old friend or entertaining hundreds of guests, everyone is sure to enjoy these variations of favorite tall cold ones.

Glory Days Cooler

1 cup frozen strawberries, thawed
2 ½ cups MOTT'S® apple juice
1 2-liter bottle Canada Dry® Ginger Ale

In a blender, combine 1 cup frozen strawberries and MOTT'S® apple juice until smooth. Pour into 4 tall glasses and fill each with chilled Canada Dry® Ginger Ale. Makes 4 servings.

Raspberry Ale

2 cups Canada Dry® Ginger Ale
ice
juice from 1 lime
½ teaspoon sugar
fresh or frozen raspberries

Pour 1 cup Canada Dry® Ginger Ale in each of two glasses over ice. Add juice from ½ lime and ¼ teaspoon sugar to each. Stir. Garnish with raspberries. Makes 2 servings.

Kiwi Strawberry Ale

4 kiwis, sliced (2 peeled)
1 ½ cups strawberry nectar
2 teaspoons sugar
ice
2 cups Canada Dry® Ginger Ale

Mix peeled kiwis, nectar, and sugar in blender. Pour into 2 glasses over ice and top with Canada Dry® Ginger Ale. Stir. Garnish with remaining kiwi slices. Makes 2 servings.

Cranberry-Lime Sparkle

1 cup cranberry juice
ice
1 cup Canada Dry® Club Soda
juice from 2 limes
lime slices

Pour ½ cup cranberry juice in each of two glasses over ice. Fill glasses with Canada Dry® Club Soda and top with fresh lime juice. Stir. Garnish with lime slices. Makes 2 servings.

Melon Berry Sparkle

1 ½ cups fresh watermelon chunks
1 ½ cups fresh strawberries, halved and topped
2 teaspoons sugar
ice
2 cups Canada Dry® Ginger Ale
fresh strawberries

Combine watermelon, strawberries, and sugar in blender. Blend until smooth. Pour mixture over ice and fill glass with Canada Dry® Ginger Ale. Garnish with a fresh strawberry. Makes 2 servings.

Plum Sparkle

4 plums, peeled, pitted, and cut in chunks
2 teaspoons sugar
ice
1 cup pineapple juice
1 cup Canada Dry® Ginger Ale
maraschino cherries

In blender, combine plums and sugar. Blend until smooth. Pour evenly over ice in two tall glasses. Add ½ cup pineapple juice to each. Top with Canada Dry® Ginger Ale. Stir. Garnish with a maraschino cherry. Makes 2 servings.

Blueberry Fizz

2 cups fresh blueberries
ice
2 cups Canada Dry® Ginger Ale
2 whole strawberries

Puree blueberries in blender. Pour evenly in two tall glasses over ice. Fill glasses with Canada Dry® Ginger Ale. Garnish with whole strawberry. Makes 2 servings.

Tonic and Orange Juice

1 cup orange juice
ice
2 cups Schweppes® Tonic Water
lime slices

Pour orange juice into each of two tall glasses over ice. Top with Schweppes® Tonic Water. Garnish with fresh lime slices. Makes 2 servings.

Raspberry Sparkle

2 cups fresh raspberries
2 teaspoons sugar
ice
2 cups 7 UP®

Set aside 4–6 raspberries. Puree remaining raspberries and sugar in blender. Pour in parfait glasses over ice and top with 7 UP®. Garnish with fresh raspberries. Makes 2 servings.

Risky Business

    1 cup frozen raspberries, thawed
    2 ½ cups pineapple juice
    Canada Dry® Ginger Ale
    pineapple chunks

In a blender, mix raspberries and pineapple juice until smooth. Pour into 4 tall glasses and fill each with chilled Canada Dry® Ginger Ale. Garnish with pineapple chunk on toothpick. Makes 4 servings.

Fruit Drink

    ¼ cup strawberry nectar
    ½ cup MOTT'S apple juice
    ¼ cup pineapple juice
    Canada Dry® Ginger Ale
    ice
    strawberries

Mix first three ingredients. Pour fruit juice mix into tall glasses over ice, filling each about ½ full. Add Canada Dry® Ginger Ale until full. Stir. Garnish with fresh strawberries. Makes 2 servings.

Tropical Sparkle

ice
½ cup mango nectar
½ cup pineapple juice
1 cup 7 UP®
fresh pineapple chunks

Fill glasses with ice. Pour ¼ cup mango nectar and ¼ cup pineapple juice in each glass. Fill glasses with 7 UP® and stir. Garnish with fresh pineapple chunks on toothpick. Makes 2 servings.

Bit o' the Bubbly

ice
juice from 1 lime
4 tablespoons sugar
1 ½ cups Canada Dry® Club Soda
lime slices

Fill two small glasses with ice. Add juice from ½ lime and 2 tablespoons sugar to each glass. Fill glasses with Canada Dry® Club Soda. Stir well. Garnish with lime slice. Makes 2 servings.

Strawberry Sparkle

1 cup strawberry nectar
1 cup Canada Dry® Ginger Ale
4 teaspoons lime juice
ice
lime slices

Combine first three ingredients. Pour into two tall glasses over ice. Garnish with fresh lime slices. Makes 2 servings.

Strawberry Sunrise

½ cup orange juice
½ cup strawberry nectar
Canada Dry® Ginger Ale
fresh strawberries

Combine juice and nectar. Stir well. Pour ½ cup of mixture in each of 2 glasses over ice. Fill glasses with Canada Dry® Ginger Ale. Garnish each with fresh strawberry. Makes 2 servings.

The Nutty Refresher

1 quart iced tea, strongly brewed
2 6-ounce cans frozen lemonade concentrate,
    thawed
2 6-ounce cans water
1 tablespoon almond extract
1 teaspoon vanilla
8 cups cold water
ice
lemon slices

Mix first six ingredients. Serve in tall glasses over ice.
Garnish each with ½ lemon slice. Serves 2.

Seabreeze

1 cup cranberry juice
ice
2 teaspoons lemon juice
½ cup Schweppes® Tonic Water
lemon slices

Pour ½ cup cranberry juice over ice in each of two tall
glasses. Add 1 teaspoon lemon juice to each. Top with
Schweppes® Tonic Water. Stir. Garnish with lemon slices.
Makes 2 servings.

Ginger Fizz

    ice
    1 cup lemonade
    1 cup fruit punch
    splash of MOTT'S® apple juice
    Canada Dry® Ginger Ale
    strawberries

Over ice, combine lemonade, fruit punch, and
MOTT'S® apple juice in two tall glasses. Pour Canada
Dry® Ginger Ale into each glass and garnish with straw-
berries. Makes 2 servings.

Apricot-Coconut Cooler

    4 ½ cups apricot nectar
    2 cups coconut cream
    2 cups Canada Dry® Club Soda
    ⅓ cup lime juice
    ice
    lime slices

Combine first four ingredients in large pitcher with ice.
Serve in tall glasses over ice and garnish with lime slices.
Makes 6–8 servings.

Strawberry Sparkle

1 ½ cups Canada Dry® Ginger Ale
½ cup strawberry nectar
ice
fresh strawberries

Combine Canada Dry® Ginger Ale and strawberry nectar. Pour mixture over ice in two small glasses. Garnish each with fresh strawberry. Makes 2 servings.

Summer Mint Tea

2 tea bags
2 tablespoons crushed mint
4 cups boiling water
1 cup sugar
½ cup lemon juice
4 cups cold water

Steep tea and mint in 2 cups boiling water for 5 minutes. Remove tea bags. Add remaining 2 cups water, sugar, and lemon juice and heat until sugar is dissolved. Add 4 cups cold water. Chill. Serve in tall glasses over ice. Garnish with lemon slices. Makes 6–8 servings.

Juicy Fruit

1 cup MOTT'S® apple juice
½ cup orange juice
¼ cup lemon juice
⅛ cup sugar
ice
orange slices

Combine first four ingredients. Chill. Serve in glasses over ice. Garnish with orange slice. Makes 2 servings.

Strawberry Tea

3–4 tea bags
1 ½ quarts water
5–6 cups strawberry nectar
1 tablespoon sugar
ice
lemon slices

Steep tea bags in boiling water about 5-10 minutes. Let cool. In large pitcher, combine tea, nectar, and sugar over ice. Stir until well blended. Garnish with fresh lemon slice. Makes 10–12 servings.

Mango Tea

    3–4 tea bags
    1 ½ quarts water
    5–6 cups mango nectar
    2 tablespoons lemon juice
    1 tablespoon sugar
    ice
    lemon slices

Steep tea bags in boiling water 5–10 minutes. Let cool. In large pitcher, combine tea, nectar, lemon juice, and sugar over ice. Stir until well blended. Garnish with fresh lemon slice. Makes 10–12 servings.

Mr. O's The King of Swing

    3–4 tea bags
    1 ½ quarts water
    6 cups lemonade, chilled
    1 tablespoon sugar
    ice
    lemon slices

Steep tea bags in boiling water. Let cool. In large pitcher, combine tea, lemonade, and sugar over ice. Stir until well blended. Garnish with fresh lemon slices. Makes 10–12 servings.

Sweet Home Alabama Lemonade

4 cups water, chilled
juice from 8 lemons
1 cup sugar
ice
lemon slices

Combine water, lemon juice, and sugar in a pitcher. Stir until well mixed. Pour in two glasses over ice. Garnish with fresh lemon slices. Makes 8 servings.

Sparkling Lemonade

½ cup sugar
½ cup lemon juice
2 ½ cups Canada Dry® Sparkling Water
ice
lemon slices
maraschino cherries

Dissolve sugar in lemon juice. Add sugar mixture and Canada Dry® Sparkling Water in two glasses. Serve over ice. Garnish with lemon slice and maraschino cherry. Makes 2 servings.

Pineapple Lemonade

2 cups sugar
2 cups water
juice of 4 lemons
2 cups pineapple juice
ice
Canada Dry® Sparkling Water
lemon slices

Boil sugar and water until sugar is dissolved. Let cool. Add lemon and pineapple juice. Pour about ⅓ cup juice mixture in tall glasses over ice. Fill glasses with Canada Dry® Sparkling Water. Garnish each with a slice of lemon. Makes 8 servings

Sparkling Limeade

½ cup sugar
½ cup lime juice
2 ½ cups Canada Dry® Sparkling Water
ice
lime slices
maraschino cherries

Dissolve sugar in lime juice in a pitcher. Add Canada Dry® Sparkling Water. Pour into tall glasses over ice. Garnish with lime slice and maraschino cherry. Makes 3–4 servings.

Strawberry Lemonade

6 cups fresh strawberries

¾ cup sugar

3 cups cold water

¾ cup freshly squeezed lemon juice

2 cups Canada Dry® Club Soda

lemon slices

ice

Blend strawberries, sugar, and water until smooth. Stir in lemon juice. Blend in Canada Dry® Club Soda. Serve in tall glasses over ice and garnish with lemon slices. Makes 6 servings.

Mango Lemonade

3 cups mango nectar

¾ cup sugar

3 cups cold water

¾ cup freshly squeezed lemon juice

2 cups Canada Dry® Club Soda

lemon slices

ice

Blend mango nectar, sugar, and water until smooth. Stir in lemon juice and Canada Dry® Club Soda. Serve in tall glasses over ice and garnish with lemon slices. Makes 6 servings.

Linda's Lemonade

  8 cups chilled lemonade
  4 scoops lemon sherbet
  1 2-liter bottle Canada Dry® Ginger Ale

Combine 1 cup lemonade and 1 scoop sherbet in eight tall glasses. Stir slightly. Fill glass with Canada Dry® Ginger Ale. Makes 8 servings.

Cherry Limeade

  1 cup sugar
  1 cup boiling water
  1 cup lime juice
  1 ½ cups maraschino cherry juice
  1 cup Canada Dry® Club Soda
  ice
  lime slices
  maraschino cherries

Dissolve sugar in boiling water. Add lime juice, cherry juice, and Canada Dry® Club Soda. Pour into glasses over ice. Garnish with ½ lime slice and maraschino cherry. Makes 4 servings.

City Slicker Starter

    1 46-ounce tomato juice, chilled
    3 tablespoons vinegar
    ½ teaspoon onion salt
    ½ tablespoon celery salt
    ½ teaspoon seasoned salt
    ½ teaspoon pepper
    1 tablespoon Worcestershire sauce
    2 tablespoons sugar
    dash of hot pepper to taste

Combine all ingredients and chill. Serve with assorted vegetable sticks as stirs: celery, carrots, zucchini, yellow squash, asparagus, or cucumber. Makes 8–12 small servings.

Tomato Juice Cocktail

    2 ½ cups tomato juice
    juice from 1 lemon
    ½ teaspoon seasoned salt
    1 teaspoon ketchup
    ⅛ teaspoon curry powder
    ½ teaspoon paprika
    1 tablespoon Worcestershire sauce
    dash of hot pepper sauce
    1 teaspoon brown sugar
    ice
    cucumber and celery sticks

Combine first nine ingredients and chill overnight. Serve in small glasses over ice with cucumber and celery sticks for stirs. Makes 3–4 small servings

Cocoa Pepper

2 ½ cups cold Dr Pepper®
1 ½ cups cold milk
3 tablespoons instant cocoa mix
ice
whipped cream
chocolate sprinkles

Combine first three ingredients and mix well. Pour into glasses over ice. Garnish with whipped cream and chocolate sprinkles. Makes 2 servings.

Goody Two Shoes Sparkle

¾ cup orange juice
½ cup Canada Dry® Club Soda
ice
1 tablespoon grenadine
maraschino cherries

Pour orange juice and Canada Dry® Club Soda into tall glasses over ice. Add grenadine and allow to settle on bottom of glass. Top with cherry. Makes 2 servings.

Fresh Fruit Sparkle

1 cup Canada Dry® Ginger Ale
1 cup pineapple juice
1 6-ounce can frozen orange juice concentrate,
  thawed
2 cups fresh pineapple chunks
2 cups honeydew melon balls
2 cups cantaloupe balls
2 cups strawberries, halved
fresh mint sprigs

Combine Canada Dry® Ginger Ale, pineapple juice, and orange juice concentrate in blender. Blend until thoroughly mixed. Chill. Spoon fresh fruit into tall frosty mugs and fill glasses with Canada Dry® Ginger Ale mixture. Garnish with fresh mint sprigs. Makes 8–12 servings.

Pink Satin Sparkle

3 cups pineapple juice
1 ½ cups Canada Dry® Ginger Ale
¼ cup grenadine
¼ cup freshly squeezed lemon juice
ice

Combine first four ingredients and shake until well mixed. Serve in small glasses over ice. Makes 4–6 servings.

Chilled Mocha

2 squares milk chocolate
¼ cup sugar
1 ½ tablespoons coffee grounds
1 teaspoon cinnamon
¼ teaspoon nutmeg
1 cup water
3 cups milk
ice
whipped cream
chocolate sprinkles

Combine first six ingredients in saucepan and simmer. Stir until chocolate melts. Bring to boil. Add 3 cups milk and blend with whisk. Let cool. Serve in chilled mugs over ice and garnish with whipped cream and chocolate sprinkles. Makes 4 servings.

Pretty Woman

1 tablespoon lemon juice
½ cup pineapple juice
½ cup orange juice
2 cups Canada Dry® Ginger Ale
crushed ice
watermelon balls
fresh mint sprigs

Combine juices and Canada Dry® Ginger Ale. Stir well. Serve over ice in tall glasses. Garnish with watermelon balls and mint sprigs. Makes 2 servings.

Grapefruit Juicy Fruit

2 cups fresh strawberries, chopped
½ cup sugar
1 12-ounce can frozen lemonade concentrate,
    thawed
1 cup pink grapefruit juice
1 ½ cups Canada Dry® Club Soda
ice

Mix 1 cup strawberries, sugar, lemonade, and grapefruit juice. Chill. Just before serving, add Canada Dry® Club Soda and ice. Serve in tall glasses and garnish with remaining strawberries. Makes 6–8 servings.

Orange Mint

2 ½ cups water
2 cups sugar
2 grated orange rinds
2 cups fresh mint leaves
juice from 2 oranges
juice from 6 lemons
ice
1 liter Canada Dry® Ginger Ale

Boil water and sugar until sugar dissolves. Add grated orange rind and mint leaves. Simmer about 10–15 minutes. Strain. Add juices to mixture and refrigerate. When ready to serve, pour ¼ cup mixture in glass, and fill glass with ice and Canada Dry® Ginger Ale. Makes 4 servings.

The Grape Gatsby

¾ cup strawberry nectar
¼ cup grape juice
¼ teaspoon sugar
ice
2 cups Canada Dry® Ginger Ale
fresh strawberries

Combine nectar, grape juice, and sugar. Mix well. Pour about ½ cup mixture into tall glasses over ice and fill glass with Canada Dry® Ginger Ale. Garnish with fresh strawberry. Makes 2 servings.

Sparkling Pink Cadillac

¼ cup sugar
1 cup water
1 ½ cups cranberry juice
1 cup pineapple juice
1 ½ cups orange juice
2 cups 7 UP®
ice
orange slices

Boil sugar and water until sugar dissolves. Let cool. Slowly stir in juices and chill. Just before serving, add 7 UP®. Serve in tall glasses over ice and garnish with orange slices. Makes 6 servings.

Fruit Spritzer

1 ½ cups fruit juice or nectar (any flavor)
½ cup Canada Dry® Club Soda
ice
maraschino cherries

Combine first two ingredients and mix well. Serve in tall glasses over ice. Garnish with maraschino cherry. Makes 2 servings.

Orange Mint Refresher

2 ½ cups water
2 cups sugar
juice of 2–3 oranges
juice of 6 lemons
½ cup fresh mint sprigs
crushed ice
Canada Dry® Ginger Ale
orange slices
mint sprigs

Combine first five ingredients in large saucepan and steep for about 1 hour. Remove mint before serving. To serve, fill glasses with crushed ice and about ⅓ full with orange-mint mixture. Add Canada Dry® Ginger Ale. Garnish with orange slice and mint sprig. Makes 6 servings.

Apple Fizz

1 cup MOTT'S® apple juice
1 cup Canada Dry® Ginger Ale
ice cubes
maraschino cherries

Pour ½ cup MOTT'S® apple juice and ½ cup Canada Dry® Ginger Ale over ice in each glass. Stir. Garnish with maraschino cherry. Makes 2 servings.

Orange Lemon Ale

1 cup water
1 cup sugar
½ cup lemon juice
1 cup orange juice
ice
1 2-liter bottle Canada Dry® Ginger Ale
orange slices

Bring water to boil and stir in sugar. Let cool. Add juices to sugar water and chill. When ready to serve, pour about ½ cup juice mixture over ice in each glass. Fill glasses with Canada Dry® Ginger Ale. Garnish with fresh orange slices. Makes 4 servings.

Simply Irresistible Sparkle

½ cup orange juice
¼ cup strawberry nectar
¼ cup peach nectar
2 tablespoons lime juice
ice
½ cup 7 UP®
lime slices

Mix juices and nectar thoroughly. Pour ½ cup each into two ice-filled glasses and fill each with 7 UP®. Garnish with lime slices. Makes 2 servings.

Summer Breeze

ice
1 cup Canada Dry® Ginger Ale
1 cup chilled sparkling white grape juice
splash of lime juice
lime slices

Fill two glasses each with ice and add ½ cup Canada Dry® Ginger Ale and ½ cup sparkling white grape juice. Top each with a splash of lime juice. Garnish with lime slices. Makes 2 servings.

Cranberry Spritzer

 1 cup cranberry juice
 ½ cup sparkling white grape juice
 ice
 splash of Canada Dry® Club Soda
 lemon slices

Pour ½ cup cranberry juice and ¼ cup sparkling white grape juice over ice in each of two large wine glasses. Add a splash of Canada Dry® Club Soda. Garnish with lemon slices. Makes 2 servings.

Tickled Pink

 6 cups cranberry juice
 3 cups 7 UP®, chilled
 ½ cup strawberries
 ice cubes
 fresh strawberries

In large pitcher, combine first three ingredients with ice cubes. Garnish glasses with fresh strawberries. Makes 8–10 servings.

Tall Cool One

  3 tea bags
  1 quart boiling water
  ¼ cup sugar
  1 quart lemonade
  1 liter bottle Canada Dry® Ginger Ale
  ice
  fresh lemon slices

Place tea bags in boiling water and steep 5–10 minutes. Remove tea bags and stir in sugar. Add lemonade and refrigerate for 1–2 hours until chilled. Just before serving, add 1 liter of Canada Dry® Ginger Ale. Pour in tall glasses over ice and garnish with fresh lemon slices. Makes 12 servings.

Mango Lemon Cooler

  4 teaspoons instant tea
  4 tablespoons sugar
  1 ½ cups mango nectar
  ½ cup cold water
  1 6-ounce can lemonade concentrate, thawed
  3 cups Canada Dry® Ginger Ale
  ice
  lemon slices

Mix tea, sugar, mango nectar, and water. Stir until sugar and tea dissolve. Add lemonade and slowly stir in Canada Dry® Ginger Ale. Serve in tall glasses over ice. Garnish with lemon slices. Makes 6–8 servings.

Stayin' Alive Spritzer

1 cup 7 UP®
1 cup pineapple juice
½ cup grapefruit juice
½ cup orange juice
ice
maraschino cherries

Mix first four ingredients and serve in glasses over ice. Garnish each glass with maraschino cherry. Makes 2 servings.

Stardust

½ cup cranberry juice
½ cup grapefruit juice
½ cup Canada Dry® Ginger Ale
1 teaspoons sugar
ice
lime slices

Mix first four ingredients and serve in glasses over ice. Garnish with lime slices. Makes 2 servings.

CHAPTER

6

Mocktails

E specially created for festive occasions, these alcohol-
free cocktails will save the day for those certain situ-
ations when you find yourself entertaining guests who
prefer nonalcoholic versions of their favorite cocktails.
These completely alcohol-free variations of the classics
are combined with a few new surprises to give your
guests the gift of choosing from a variety of "mocktails."

Strawberry Daiquiri

2 cups fresh strawberries
1 ½ cups strawberry nectar
½ cup Canada Dry® Ginger Ale
juice of 1 lemon
1 tablespoon sugar
1 cup crushed ice
fresh strawberries

Combine strawberries, nectar, Canada Dry® Ginger Ale, lemon juice, sugar, and ice in blender. Blend until slushy. Serve in specialty glasses and garnish with fresh strawberry. Makes 2 servings.

Peach Daiquiri

3 fresh peaches, peeled, halved, and pitted
1 cup water
1 tablespoon sugar
½ cup prepared daiquiri mix
1 tablespoon rum flavoring, optional
½ cup apple juice
ice
maraschino cherries

Blend first seven ingredients until slushy and smooth. Serve in specialty glasses and garnish with maraschino cherry. Makes about 4 servings.

Banana Daiquiri

2 ripe bananas
1 cup water
1 tablespoon sugar
½ cup prepared daiquiri mix
1 tablespoon rum flavoring, optional
½ cup orange juice
ice
orange slices

Blend first seven ingredients until slushy and smooth. Serve in specialty glasses and garnish with orange slices. Makes about 4 servings.

Apple Daiquiri

1 12-ounce can frozen apple juice, thawed
2 cans water
½ cup prepared daiquiri mix
3 fresh apples, cored and peeled
1 tablespoon rum flavoring, optional
ice
maraschino cherries

Blend first six ingredients until smooth and serve in specialty glasses. Garnish with maraschino cherries. Makes 4–6 servings.

Señorita Margarita

½ cup Canada Dry® Club Soda
2 cups margarita mix
4 cups crushed ice
2 teaspoons lime juice
2 teaspoons salt, optional
lime slices

Mix first four ingredients in blender until slushy. Serve in margarita glasses with salt around rim, if desired. Garnish with fresh lime slice. Makes 2 servings.

Strawberry Margarita

4 cups fresh strawberries, halved
1 cup sweet and sour mix
4 cups crushed ice
2 tablespoons lime juice
2 whole strawberries

Blend first four ingredients until slushy. Serve in margarita glass with whole strawberry to garnish. Makes 2 servings.

Poinsettias

    1 cup nonalcoholic champagne
    1 cup cranberry juice
    ice
    maraschino cherries

Mix champagne and cranberry juice in blender. Chill. Serve in wine glasses over ice and garnish with a maraschino cherry. Makes 2 servings.

Sangria Blanca

    ½ cup water
    ½ cup sugar
    3 lemons, sliced
    3 oranges, sliced
    3 limes, sliced
    1 bottle nonalcoholic white wine
    2 cups chilled Canada Dry® Club Soda
    crushed ice

Boil water. Add sugar and stir until it dissolves. Place most of fruit slices in bottom of large glass pitcher. Pour sugar-water mixture over ice. Add nonalcoholic wine, Canada Dry® Club Soda, and crushed ice. Mix well. Serve in glasses garnished with ½ fruit slice. Makes 12 servings.

Mia Sangria

    1 12-ounce can frozen pink lemonade concentrate,
        thawed
    4 cups grape juice
    juice of 1 lime
    2 cups Canada Dry® Club Soda
    lemon slices
    lime slices

Combine lemonade, grape juice, and lime juice. Stir. Slowly stir in Canada Dry® Club Soda. Garnish with lemon and lime slices. Makes 6–8 servings.

White Sangria

    1 bottle nonalcoholic white wine
    1 liter Canada Dry® Club soda
    1 cup orange juice
    ⅓ cup sugar
    crushed ice
    lemon slices
    lime slices

Combine first five ingredients in clear glass pitcher. Mix well. Garnish with floating fruit. Makes 8 servings.

½ litre Red wine
½ " Cranberry Juice
1 cup Club Soda   Excellent
3 Tbs Sugar
Lemon Slices.

Like a Virgin Bloody Mary

- 1 46-ounce can tomato juice
- 1 6-ounce can frozen orange juice
    concentrate, thawed
- 3 6-ounce cans cold water
- ¼ cup Worcestershire sauce
- ¼ tablespoon horseradish
- juice of 1 lemon
- 1 teaspoon salt
- dash of hot pepper sauce
- celery sticks

Mix first eight ingredients together in a large pitcher. Serve in small glasses with celery sticks for stirs. Makes 8 servings.

Mock Bloody Mary

- 1 46-ounce can tomato juice, chilled
- 2 tablespoons lemon juice
- ¼ teaspoon hot pepper sauce
- 1 tablespoon Worcestershire sauce
- dash of ground red pepper
- ice
- celery sticks

Mix first five ingredients together and pour in glasses over ice. Use celery sticks for garnish. Makes 8 servings.

Mock Julep

¼ cup sugar
½ cup cold water
juice from 1 lemon
2 mint leaves
ice
1 ½ cups Canada Dry® Ginger Ale
lemon slices

Mix sugar, water, and lemon juice. Add mint leaves and let stand about 1 hour. Serve in two ice-filled glasses and top with Canada Dry® Ginger Ale. Garnish with lemon slice. Makes 2 servings.

Nonalcoholic Texas Tumbleweed

½ cup strong coffee
1 tablespoon vanilla
6–8 scoops vanilla ice cream
whipped cream
chocolate shavings

Combine first three ingredients in blender just until mixed. Pour in parfait glasses to serve. Top with whipped cream and chocolate shavings. Makes 8 servings.

Tommy Collins

1 cup Canada Dry® Club Soda
juice of 1 lemon
2 teaspoons powdered sugar
crushed ice
lemon slice

Shake ½ cup Canada Dry® Club Soda, lemon juice, and sugar in a container with ice until well mixed. Strain over crushed ice in a tall glass. Fill glass with remaining Canada Dry® Club Soda. Garnish with lemon slice. Makes 1 serving.

Almosta Mimosa

½ cup orange juice
½ cup Canada Dry® Ginger Ale
ice
orange slice

Combine orange juice and Canada Dry® Ginger Ale over ice. Stir. Serve with a fresh orange slice. Makes 1 serving.

Virgin Piña Colada

½ cup cream of coconut
1 ½ cups chilled pineapple juice
2 ½ cups crushed ice
¼ cup Canada Dry® Club Soda
pineapple chunks

In blender, combine first four ingredients and blend on high for about 30 seconds or until slushy. Pour into chilled glasses. Garnish with fresh pineapple chunks on toothpicks. Makes 4 servings.

Little Shirley Temple

ice
1 dash grenadine
¾ cup Canada Dry® Ginger Ale
maraschino cherry

Fill tall glass with ice. Add grenadine. Top with Canada Dry® Ginger Ale and garnish with maraschino cherry. Makes 1 serving.

Fuzzy-Wuzzy Navel

¾ cup orange juice
¼ cup peach nectar
ice
orange slice

Combine orange juice and peach nectar in tall glass over ice. Stir gently. Garnish with fresh orange slice. Makes 1 serving.

Sparkling Lone Star

¼ cup Cananda Dry® Ginger Ale
½ cup orange juice
ice
splash of lemon juice
splash of grenadine
maraschino cherry

Pour Cananda Dry® Ginger Ale and orange juice over ice in small glass. Splash with lemon juice and grenadine. Garnish with maraschino cherry. Makes 1 serving.

Dustcutter

¼ cup lime juice
ice
2 cups Canada Dry® Tonic Water
lime slice

In a tall glass, pour lime juice over ice and top off with Canada Dry® Tonic Water. Garnish with fresh lime slice. Makes 1 serving.

Weekend Fling

1 ½ cups lemonade
3 tablespoons coconut cream
ice
grated coconut
fresh cherries

Combine lemonade and coconut cream in blender. Blend on high for about 10 seconds. Pour over ice in a specialty glass. Sprinkle with grated coconut and garnish with fresh cherry. Makes 2 servings.

The Dancing Queen

½ cup MOTT'S® apple juice
½ cup cranberry juice
splash of pineapple juice
ice
2 tablespoons Canada Dry® Sparkling Water
maraschino cherries
pineapple chunks

Combine juices. Pour over ice in tall glass. Add Canada Dry® Sparkling Water to fill glass. Stir. Garnish with maraschino cherries and pineapple chunks on toothpick. Makes 1 serving.

CHAPTER

7

Holiday Treats

Throughout the year, there are countless occasions for celebration. Official holidays account for only a few, but there are many other special occasions you just can't miss. Whether you are celebrating with just your sweetheart or a large group of friends, be sure you have the edge on the new holiday classics.

New Year's Punch (New Year's Eve)

  2 bottles nonalcoholic champagne
  1 quart Canada Dry® Ginger Ale
  ice
  strawberries
  orange slices
  lemon slices

Add champagne and Canada Dry® Ginger Ale to punch bowl over ice. Garnish with fruit. Makes 12 servings.

Sweetheart Sparkle (Valentine's Day)

  2 tablespoons powdered sugar
  ½ cup grapefruit juice
  1 ½ cups Canada Dry® Ginger Ale
  ice
  candied hearts

Stir powdered sugar into juice until thoroughly mixed. Add Canada Dry® Ginger Ale and stir. Pour in glasses over ice. Garnish with candied hearts. Makes 2 servings.

Masquerade Punch (Mardi Gras)

1 10-ounce package frozen raspberries, thawed
3 cups Canada Dry® Club Soda
3 cups Canada Dry® Ginger Ale
1 cup cranberry juice
1 12-ounce can frozen pink lemonade
ice
orange slices

Combine first five ingredients in a punch bowl. Mix well. Gently add ice and garnish with orange slices. Makes about 18 servings.

St. Paddy's Refresher (St. Patrick's Day)

2 ½ cups crushed ice
1 6-ounce can frozen limeade concentrate, thawed
¼ cup lemon juice
2 ½ cups Canada Dry® Club Soda
mint sprigs
lime slices
green food coloring, optional

Combine first four ingredients in pitcher. Garnish with mint sprigs and lime slices. Tint beverage a darker shade of green with green food coloring, if desired. Makes 4 servings.

Bunny Hop Punch (Easter)

1 package instant lemon-flavored drink mix
1 package instant lime-flavored drink mix
2 cups sugar
1 quart water
1 46-ounce can pineapple juice
1 cup crushed pineapple
1 small can frozen lemonade concentrate, thawed
3 cans cold water
1 quart lemon-lime sherbet
1 2-liter bottle Canada Dry® Ginger Ale

Mix instant drink mixes, sugar, and water. Add pineapple juice and pineapple. Add lemonade and 3 cans cold water. Pour into freezer bags and freeze. When ready to serve, place in punch bowl and thaw until slushy. Gently add sherbet over slush and stir in Canada Dry® Ginger Ale. Makes about 24 servings.

April Fool's! (April Fool's Day)

1 2-liter bottle Canada Dry® Ginger Ale
1 46-ounce can pineapple juice
1 16-ounce bottle cranberry juice
1 quart water
1 ½ cups sugar
1 6-ounce can frozen lemonade concentrate,
    thawed
lemon slices

Pour about 1 liter of Canada Dry® Ginger Ale into ice cube trays. (For an April Fool's Day trick, place a plastic bug in one of the ice cube trays.) Freeze. Chill juices. Boil water and sugar together until sugar dissolves. Chill. Combine juices and sugar-water mixture in punch bowl over Canada Dry® Ginger Ale ice cubes. Slowly stir in about 1 liter of Canada Dry® Ginger Ale. Garnish with fresh lemon slices. Makes about 32 servings.

Fiesta Punch (Cinco de Mayo)

3 cups Canada Dry® Club Soda
2 ¼ quarts margarita mix
¼ cup lime juice
⅛ cup salt
3–4 quarts crushed ice
lime slices
salt, optional

Mix first four ingredients in large punch bowl over ice. Float fresh lime slices in punch bowl to garnish. Serve in mini-margarita glasses with salt around rim, if desired. Makes 24 punch-size servings.

Fruit Sparkler (Fourth of July)

½ cup crushed ice
12 fresh blueberries
12 fresh raspberries
1 cup Canada Dry® Ginger Ale

In tall glass, layer ⅛ cup crushed ice, 6 blueberries, ⅛ cup ice, 6 raspberries, and remaining ice. Fill glass with Canada Dry® Ginger Ale and top with remaining raspberries and blueberries. Makes 1 serving.

Independence Day Cooler (Fourth of July)

2 cups grape juice
2 cups cranberry juice
1 liter Canada Dry® Club Soda
ice
lemon slices

Combine first three ingredients and chill. Serve over ice and garnish with lemon slices. Makes about 8 servings.

Yankee Doodle Drink (Fourth of July)

8 lemon wedges
4 cinnamon sticks
4 whole cloves
2 cups MOTT'S® apple juice
2 tablespoons maple syrup
ice cubes
2 cups Canada Dry® Club Soda, chilled

Combine 4 lemon wedges, cinnamon sticks, cloves, MOTT'S® apple juice, and syrup in saucepan and simmer about 10–15 minutes. Place in refrigerator and chill. Pour about ½ cup in tall glasses over ice and fill each glass with Canada Dry® Club Soda. Garnish with remaining lemon wedges. Makes 4 servings.

Trick or Treat Punch (Halloween)

1 liter Canada Dry® Ginger Ale
1 6-ounce can frozen orange juice concentrate,
    thawed
3 cans water
1 pint orange sherbet
black licorice bits

Mix Canada Dry® Ginger Ale, orange juice, and water. Chill. To serve, place one scoop of sherbet in each glass. Fill glass with mixture. Garnish with black licorice bits. Makes about 8 servings.

Thanksgiving Spice (Thanksgiving)

2 cups pineapple juice
1 ½ cups apricot nectar
2 cups MOTT'S® apple juice
½ cup orange juice
½ tablespoon cinnamon
¼ teaspoon salt
½ teaspoon whole cloves

Pour juices into electric percolator. Place spices in basket and perk. Serve in hot mugs. (If you're not using a percolator, pour juices in large saucepan on stove and add spices. Simmer 10–15 minutes. Remove cloves with slotted spoon and serve.) Makes 6 servings.

Santa's Surprise Punch (Christmas)

maraschino cherries
1 2-liter bottle Canada Dry® Ginger Ale
1 46-ounce can pineapple juice
1 6-ounce can frozen orange juice concentrate,
    thawed.
½ teaspoon peppermint extract

Place one cherry in each cube of ice tray and fill with Canada Dry® Ginger Ale. Freeze overnight. Combine chilled juices in punch bowl. Add peppermint extract and stir. Pour in remaining Canada Dry® Ginger Ale and add Canada Dry® Ginger Ale ice cubes. Makes 16 servings.

Eggnog (Christmas)

8 eggs
3 cups sugar
1 tablespoon rum flavoring
2 pints whipped cream
2 quarts commercial eggnog
½ gallon milk
¼ teaspoon vanilla

Whip eggs and sugar until fluffy. Add rum flavoring. Pour egg mixture over whipped cream and beat. Slowly add eggnog, milk, and vanilla. Stir well. Makes about 24 servings.

Chocolate Eggnog (Christmas)

3 cups prepared eggnog, chilled
1 cup milk
2 tablespoons chocolate syrup
2 tablespoons powdered sugar
2 cups whipped cream
chocolate shavings

Combine eggnog, milk, and chocolate syrup in pitcher. Stir until well mixed. Cover and chill. Mix powdered sugar and one cup whipped cream. Serve in cups topped with remaining whipped cream and chocolate shavings. Makes 4 servings.

Dr Pepper® Eggnog (Christmas)

1 2-liter bottle Dr Pepper®, chilled
1 quart eggnog mix
grated nutmeg

Pour some Dr Pepper® into 2 ice cube trays. Freeze overnight. Combine eggnog mix with 2 cups cold Dr Pepper® in punch bowl. Sprinkle with grated nutmeg. Add Dr Pepper® ice cubes. Makes 6–8 servings.

Party Wassail (Christmas)

1 cup brown sugar
4 broken cinnamon sticks
4 teaspoons whole cloves
9 cups cranberry juice
4 ½ cups water
8 cups MOTT'S® apple juice
1 6-ounce can frozen orange juice concentrate,
    thawed
whole cinnamon sticks

Place first three ingredients in basket of percolator. Put juices and water in the pot and perk. Serve hot in mugs with cinnamon sticks to garnish. (Without a percolator, combine first seven ingredients in large pot on stove. Simmer about 20–25 minutes. Before serving, remove cloves and cinnamon pieces with slotted spoon.) Makes 25–30 servings.

Mrs. Claus's Lemon Fizz (Christmas)

½ cup peach nectar
1 ½ cups pineapple juice
ice
2 cups Canada Dry® Ginger Ale
lemon slices

Combine peach nectar and pineapple juice. Pour 1 cup mixture in each of two tall glasses over ice. Top with chilled Canada Dry® Ginger Ale. Garnish each with lemon slice. Makes 2 servings.

Christmas Classic (Christmas)

  1 cup cranberry juice
  ½ cup pineapple juice
  ½ cup orange juice
  ice
  4 cinnamon sticks
  Canada Dry® Club Soda

Combine all juices. Pour ½ cup juice mixture over ice in each of four tall glasses. Place one cinnamon stick in each glass. Add Canada Dry® Club Soda to fill glasses and stir gently. Makes 4 servings.

CHAPTER

8

Cold Punches for Any Occasion

For the countless days throughout the year that you may find yourself entertaining, try your hand at one of these delicious party punches. They're good for any occasion and even better if you're throwing a "Just Because" party. Remember that punch servings equal about ½ cup.

Texas Two-Step Punch

1 ½ quart water
2 packages instant lemon-lime flavored drink mix
1 46-ounce can pineapple juice, chilled
1 2-liter bottle 7 UP®
ice
10 scoops lime sherbet
lime slices

Mix first four ingredients well in punch bowl. Add ice and 8–10 scoops of lime sherbet. Float lime slices on top to garnish. Makes about 36 servings.

Easy Cranberry Punch

1 48-ounce bottle cranberry juice
1 pint pineapple sherbet
1 2-liter bottle Canada Dry® Ginger Ale
fresh cranberries

Combine first three ingredients together and chill. Garnish with fresh cranberries. Makes about 26 servings.

Mocha Punch

    2 quarts milk
    ⅔ cup chocolate syrup
    1 teaspoon vanilla
    ¼ teaspoon almond extract
    ½ gallon coffee ice cream or frozen yogurt
    chocolate shavings

Combine milk and syrup and mix until well blended. Add vanilla and almond extract. Stir. Place small scoop of ice cream or yogurt in punch glasses before serving. Fill glasses with chocolate milk mixture. Garnish with chocolate shavings. Makes about 20 servings.

Raspberry Beret Punch

    2 2-liter bottles Canada Dry® Ginger Ale
    ½ gallon raspberry sherbet
    2 cups fresh raspberries

Pour about 1 liter Canada Dry® Ginger Ale into ice cube trays. Freeze overnight. Just before serving time, scoop sherbet into punch bowl and slowly add remaining Canada Dry® Ginger Ale. Gently mix until sherbet is soft. Add Canada Dry® Ginger Ale ice cubes and raspberries to garnish. Makes about 20 servings.

Sparkling Citrus Punch

1 quart orange juice
1 quart pineapple juice
1 32-ounce bottle Canada Dry® Club Soda
ice cubes
orange slices

Mix orange juice and pineapple juice in large punch bowl. Slowly stir in Canada Dry® Club Soda and stir gently. Just before serving, add ice cubes and garnish with orange slices. Makes about 24 servings.

Very Cranberry Punch

1 40-ounce bottle cranberry juice
1 quart lemonade
2 cups Canada Dry® Club Soda, chilled
fresh fruit slices
ice

Pour cranberry juice and lemonade in a punch bowl. Stir in Canada Dry® Club Soda. Garnish with fresh fruit slices. Serve over ice. Makes about 20 servings.

Stairway to Heaven Punch

3 cups sugar
2 3-ounce packages strawberry gelatin
2 quarts boiling water
1 46-ounce can pineapple juice
½ cup lemon juice
1 teaspoon vanilla
1 teaspoon almond extract
2 quarts cold water
1 2-liter bottle 7 UP®

Combine first three ingredients. Stir well and cool. Add pineapple juice, lemon juice, vanilla, almond extract, and cold water. Mix well and pour into freezer bags. Freeze overnight. When ready to serve, thaw punch until slushy. Add 7 UP®. Makes about 20 servings.

Texas Sunrise Punch

2 2-liter bottles Canada Dry® Ginger Ale
1 12-ounce can frozen orange juice concentrate, thawed
1 12-ounce can apricot nectar
1 ½ pints strawberry sherbet
3 cups water
fresh strawberries

Pour Canada Dry® Ginger Ale into four ice cube trays. Freeze overnight. Combine juices and water in large container. Stir until blended. When ready to serve, pour mixture into punch bowl. Add Canada Dry® Ginger Ale and Canada Dry® Ginger Ale ice cubes. Garnish with fresh strawberries. Makes about 26 servings.

Soda Fountain Punch

1 quart vanilla ice cream
7 cups cold Dr Pepper®

Place ice cream in bowl. When softened, beat until smooth. Gradually add 2 cups cold Dr Pepper®, beating until well mixed. Pour into punch bowl and add remaining Dr Pepper® and mix well. Makes about 20 servings.

Sunset Punch

1 46-ounce can pineapple juice
1 pint strawberry ice cream
1 pint orange sherbet
3 cups Canada Dry® Ginger Ale
orange slices

Mix juice, ice cream, and sherbet in bowl. Beat with electric mixer until well blended. Pour mixture in punch bowl and add Canada Dry® Ginger Ale. Garnish with orange slices. Makes about 26 servings.

Mon Cheri

    3 ½ cups pineapple juice
    1 package instant black-cherry flavored drink mix
    1 package instant pink lemonade flavored drink
        mix
    1 ½ cups sugar
    2 quarts water
    lemon slices

Freeze 2 cups pineapple juice in ice ring mold. Mix remaining juice with next four ingredients. Pour into large punch bowl over ice ring. Garnish with fresh lemon slices. Makes about 24 servings.

The Sundance Kid

    1 46-ounce can pineapple juice
    3 cups apricot nectar
    1 liter Canada Dry® Club Soda
    1 quart pineapple sherbet
    1 cup maraschino cherries

Combine chilled pineapple juice and apricot nectar in large punch bowl. Add chilled Canada Dry® Club Soda and sherbet just before serving. Garnish with maraschino cherries. Makes about 26 servings.

Pink Panther Punch

1 2-liter bottle Canada Dry® Ginger Ale
2 quarts pink grapefruit juice
orange slices
maraschino cherries
ice

In large punch bowl, combine Canada Dry® Ginger Ale and grapefruit juice in equal parts. Add orange slices, cherries, and ice to top of punch. Makes about 16 servings.

Sparkling Ruby Punch

crushed ice
1 6-ounce can frozen lemonade, thawed
1 6-ounce can frozen apple juice, thawed
2 cans cold water
1 quart fruit punch
1 pint cranberry juice
1 2-liter bottle 7 UP®
lemon slices

Place ice in punch bowl. Add next six ingredients, mix, and serve. Garnish with fresh lemon slices. Makes about 36 servings.

Mock Champagne Punch

1 6-ounce can frozen lemonade concentrate,
    thawed
8 cups chilled pineapple juice
2 bottles nonalcoholic white wine
1 bottle nonalcoholic champagne
crushed ice
maraschino cherries

Mix first four ingredients in punch bowl. Add crushed ice and maraschino cherries to garnish. Makes about 36 servings.

Wildcat Punch

1 2-liter bottle Canada Dry® Ginger Ale
maraschino cherries
2 quarts iced tea
1 6-ounce can frozen orange juice concentrate,
    thawed
1 6-ounce can frozen grape juice, thawed
3 tablespoons sugar
1 6-ounce can frozen lemonade, thawed
ice

Fill ice cube trays with 1 liter Canada Dry® Ginger Ale and add 1 maraschino cherry to each cube. Freeze overnight. In punch bowl, combine tea, juices, sugar, and lemonade. Just before serving, add ice and Canada Dry® Ginger Ale. Makes about 36 servings.

Celebrate Good Times Punch

    1 2-liter bottle 7 UP®
    2 6-ounce cans frozen orange juice concentrate,
        thawed
    3 ½ cups water
    2 tablespoons lime juice
    4 teaspoons rum flavoring (optional)
    orange slices
    lemon slices

Pour 7 UP® in four ice cube trays and freeze overnight.
Combine orange juice, water, lime juice, and rum flavoring in punch bowl and stir. Add remaining 7 UP® and
7 UP® ice cubes. Garnish with orange and lemon slices.
Makes about 26 servings.

Fresh 'n Fruity Punch

- 1 10-ounce package frozen strawberries, thawed
- 3 bananas, chopped
- 1 6-ounce can frozen orange juice concentrate, thawed
- 1 6-ounce can frozen lemonade concentrate, thawed
- 3 packages powdered cherry-flavored drink mix
- 2 cups sugar
- 4 quarts cold water
- ice
- 1 28-ounce bottle Canada Dry® Ginger Ale
- maraschino cherries

Combine fruits and juices in blender and blend until thoroughly mixed. In a separate large bowl, combine drink mix, sugar, and water, and stir until sugar is dissolved. Add fruit mixture and stir well. Just before serving, add ice and Canada Dry® Ginger Ale. Garnish with maraschino cherries. Makes about 40 servings.

Minty Punch

    1 ¼ cups lemon juice
    3 6-ounce cans frozen orange juice concentrate
    ⅔ cup sugar
    1 ½ cups hard peppermint candies
    1 2-liter bottle Canada Dry® Ginger Ale
    lemon slices
    candy canes

Combine lemon juice, orange juice, sugar, and candies in blender. Blend until candies dissolve. Pour in large punch bowl and add Canada Dry® Ginger Ale. Garnish with sliced lemons and candy canes. Makes about 20 servings.

Key Lime Cooler

    1 cup sugar
    4 cups cold water
    1 package instant lime-flavored drink mix
    1 46-ounce can pineapple juice
    4 cups Canada Dry® Ginger Ale
    ice
    maraschino cherries

Mix sugar and water until sugar is dissolved. Mix in lime drink mix and pineapple juice. Just before serving, add Canada Dry® Ginger Ale and ice. Garnish with maraschino cherries. Makes about 26 servings.

Bad, Bad Leroy Brown Punch

1 2-liter bottle Dr Pepper®, chilled
1 ½ cups sugar
4 cups water
½ cup lemon juice
4 cups cranberry juice
1 cup pineapple juice
¼ teaspoon salt

Pour about 1 liter Dr Pepper® into ice cube trays. Freeze overnight. Mix sugar with 2 cups water. Bring to a boil. Stir until sugar dissolves, then let cool. Add remaining 2 cups water, juices, and salt. When ready to serve, stir in cold Dr Pepper® over Dr Pepper® ice cubes in punch bowl. Makes about 32 servings.

Cranberry Fizz Punch

10 cups cranberry juice
2 oranges
2 lemons
12 sugar cubes
1 12-ounce can frozen grapefruit juice
3 cups Canada Dry® Club Soda, chilled

Freeze 3 cups of cranberry juice in ice ring. Squeeze juice from oranges and lemons. Set aside. Crush sugar cubes in bottom of large punch bowl. Place cranberry ice ring in punch bowl. Add juice from oranges, lemons, frozen grapefruit juice, and remaining cranberry juice. Mix well. Gently stir in Canada Dry® Tonic Water. Makes about 32 servings.

Island Delight Punch

2 cups pineapple chunks, with juice
1 40-ounce bottle cranapple juice
ice
1 2-liter bottle Canada Dry® Ginger Ale, chilled
ice

Combine pineapple and cranapple juice in a punch bowl. Add ice and gently stir in Canada Dry® Ginger Ale. Makes about 26 servings.

Icy Lemon-Lime Punch

1 6-ounce package lime gelatin
3 ½ cups boiling water
1 ¼ cups sugar
1 46-ounce can pineapple juice
2 6-ounce cans frozen lemonade concentrate,
    thawed
6 cups cold water
1 2-liter bottle Canada Dry® Ginger Ale
lemon slices
lime slices

Dissolve gelatin in boiling water. Add sugar, pineapple juice, lemonade, and water. Freeze in freezer bags. Partially thaw and pour in punch bowl. Add Canada Dry® Ginger Ale. Garnish with lemon and lime slices. Makes about 50 servings.

Copacabana Punch

1 2-liter bottle Canada Dry® Ginger Ale
4 cups grape juice
1 46-ounce can pineapple-grapefruit juice
maraschino cherries

Pour Canada Dry® Ginger Ale in four ice cube trays. Add 1 maraschino cherry to each cube. Freeze overnight. Combine juices and remaining Canada Dry® Ginger Ale in punch bowl and stir. Add Canada Dry® Ginger Ale ice cubes. Makes about 24 servings.

Strawberry Punch

3 6-ounce cans frozen lemonade concentrate, thawed
3 10-ounce packages frozen strawberries, thawed
1 ½ quarts Canada Dry® Ginger Ale
ice
lemon slices

In blender, mix 1 can lemonade with 2 packages strawberries. Combine remaining strawberries, lemonade, and Canada Dry® Ginger Ale in punch bowl over ice. Add blended portion and mix well. Garnish with lemon slices. Makes about 18 servings.

The Odd Couple's Perfect Punch

1 2-liter bottle Canada Dry® Ginger Ale
1 ½ cups sugar
1 quart hot tea
1 quart orange juice
1 cup freshly squeezed lemon juice
orange slices
lemon slices

Pour about 1 liter of Canada Dry® Ginger Ale into ice cube trays. Freeze until solid. Add sugar to hot tea, stirring until sugar is completely dissolved. Cool. Combine orange juice, lemon juice, and tea in punch bowl over Canada Dry® Ginger Ale ice cubes. Just before serving, add Canada Dry® Ginger Ale and fresh fruit slices to garnish. Makes about 28 servings.

Copa Banana Punch

2 cups sugar
2 cups boiling water
6 bananas, mashed
1 6-ounce can frozen orange juice concentrate,
    thawed
1 6-ounce can frozen lemonade concentrate,
    thawed
1 46-ounce can pineapple juice
8 cups water
½ cup lime juice
1 liter Canada Dry® Ginger Ale
lemon slices
orange slices
maraschino cherries

Dissolve sugar in 2 cups boiling water. Let cool. Combine next six ingredients with sugar water in freezer container. Freeze overnight. Remove from freezer about two hours before serving. Just before serving, add Canada Dry® Ginger Ale and garnish with lemon and orange slices and cherries. Makes about 40 servings.

Raspberry Punch

1 quart tea
1 cup sugar
2 packages raspberry gelatin
4 cups water
juice of 6 lemons
1 46-ounce can pineapple juice
1 6-ounce can frozen orange juice
2 10-ounce packages frozen raspberries, thawed
1 liter Canada Dry® Ginger Ale

Combine tea, sugar, gelatin, and water. Pour into punch bowl and then add fruit juices. Just before serving, add 2 packages raspberries and 1 liter Canada Dry® Ginger Ale. Makes about 30 servings.

Cinderella Punch

1 quart cran-grape juice
1 bottle sparkling nonalcoholic champagne
1 bottle nonalcoholic sparkling white wine
2 cups Canada Dry® Club Soda
cranberries

Freeze cran-grape juice in ice ring. Combine next three ingredients and chill. Serve in punch bowl over ice ring and garnish with fresh cranberries. Makes about 16 servings.

Sparkling Citrus Fizz

1 cup boiling water
2 tablespoons crushed mint
1 cup raspberry jelly
½ cup freshly squeezed lemon juice
3 cups freshly squeezed orange juice
1 cup cold water
1 quart Canada Dry® Ginger Ale, chilled
mint sprigs
orange slices
lemon slices

Combine boiling water, mint, and raspberry jelly. Stir. When well mixed, let cool. Pour chilled juices and water in punch bowl. Just before serving, add Canada Dry® Ginger Ale. Garnish with mint sprigs, orange slices, and lemon slices. Makes about 22 servings.

The Dirty Dozen

12 oranges
6 lemons
6 limes
¾ cup sugar
1 tablespoon vanilla
1 2-liter bottle 7 UP®
lime slices

Squeeze juice from oranges, lemons, and limes. Combine in large punch bowl. Slowly stir in sugar until dissolved. Add vanilla. Just before serving, add 7 UP®. Garnish with fresh lime slices. Makes about 40 servings.

Peppermint Twist Punch

¼ lb. hard peppermint candy
water
1 46-ounce can fruit punch
1 liter Canada Dry® Ginger Ale

Place 10–12 candies in mold with water and freeze overnight. Melt remaining candy in 1 cup fruit punch over medium heat until dissolved. Cool. Mix with remaining fruit punch and chill. Pour in punch bowl over ice ring. Add Canada Dry® Ginger Ale just before serving. Makes about 18 servings.

Cranberry-Lime Punch

1 2-liter bottle Canada Dry® Ginger Ale
2 quarts cranberry juice
ice
fresh cranberries
lime wedges

In large punch bowl, combine Canada Dry® Ginger Ale and cranberry juice in equal parts over ice. Add fresh cranberries and lime wedges to top of punch. Makes about 32 servings.

Fruity Summer Punch

- 1 46-ounce can pineapple juice
- 1 12-ounce can frozen orange juice concentrate, thawed
- 1 12-ounce can frozen pink lemonade, thawed
- 1 2-liter bottle Canada Dry® Ginger Ale
- 1 bottle nonalcoholic sparkling white wine
- ice
- 1 10-ounce package frozen straw-berries
- 1 small can pineapple tidbits

Mix first five ingredients in punch bowl over ice and add strawberries and pineapple. Makes about 38 servings.

Susie Q's Slush Punch

- 2 small packages orange gelatin
- 3 cups sugar
- 3 cups boiling water
- 3 cups cold water
- 1 8-ounce bottle lemon juice
- 1 46-ounce can pineapple juice
- 1 2-liter bottle Canada Dry® Ginger Ale

Mix gelatin, sugar, and boiling water until dissolved. Add cold water. Let cool, and then add lemon juice and pineapple juice. Freeze in large freezer-safe container or freezer bags overnight until icy. At serving time, pour into punch bowl and add Canada Dry® Ginger Ale. Makes about 36 servings.

Happy Days Punch

1 cup sugar
3 cups water
1 cup prepared tea
2 cups strawberry syrup
1 6-ounce can frozen orange juice
1 16-ounce can crushed pineapple
juice from 3 lemons
2 pints raspberry sherbet
1 liter Canada Dry® Club Soda

Dissolve sugar in 1 cup boiling water. Let cool. In punch bowl, add remaining water and next five ingredients. Add sherbet and cold Canada Dry® Club Soda when ready to serve. Makes about 24 servings.

Frozen Daiquiri Punch

2 cups lemon juice
4 cups orange juice
4 cups lime juice
2 cups sugar
4 cups Canada Dry® Club Soda
4 teaspoons rum flavoring
lime slices

Mix juices and sugar. Chill. Place in punch bowl and slowly add Canada Dry® Club Soda and rum flavoring. Stir. Garnish with lime slices. Makes about 24 servings.

Paradise City Punch

1 cup sugar
2 cups water
⅔ cup orange juice
2 cups pineapple juice
¼ cup lemon juice
2 cups iced tea
4 cups Canada Dry® Ginger Ale
ice

Boil sugar and water until sugar is dissolved. Add juices and tea. Just before serving, add Canada Dry® Ginger Ale and ice. Makes about 20 servings.

The Great Pretender Punch

2 packages strawberry gelatin
½ cup sugar
3 cups hot water
½ cup lemon juice
5 cups chilled Dr Pepper®
ice or Dr Pepper® ice cubes

Dissolve gelatin and sugar in hot water. Add lemon juice. Cool. Just before serving, stir in cold Dr Pepper®. Serve in punch bowl with ice or Dr Pepper® ice cubes. Makes about 16 servings.

Cherry Dr Pepper® Party Punch

    3 cups hot water
    ½ cup sugar
    2 3-ounce packages cherry gelatin
    3 cups cold water
    ½ cup lemon juice
    1 cup pineapple juice
    ⅛ teaspoon salt
    ¼ teaspoon almond extract
    5 cups chilled Dr Pepper®
    crushed ice

Combine hot water and sugar in a saucepan. Bring to a boil. Add gelatin, stirring until well dissolved. Add cold water, lemon juice, pineapple juice, salt, and extract. Cool. Just before serving, stir in Dr Pepper®. Serve with crushed ice. Makes about 24 servings.

Brunch Coffee Punch

    8 cups strong coffee
    3 cinnamon sticks
    ⅓ cup sugar
    1 pint whipped cream
    1 quart vanilla ice cream

Prepare coffee and add cinnamon sticks and sugar while coffee is still hot. Cool overnight. When ready to serve, add whipped cream and ice cream. Stir gently. Makes about 30 servings.

Slushy Punch

3 ½ cups sugar

6 cups water

2 packages mixed fruit gelatin

1 46-ounce can pineapple juice

4 cups orange juice

⅔ cup lemon juice

1 2-liter bottle Canada Dry® Ginger Ale

Bring sugar and water to boil in large pan, simmer for about 5 minutes and add gelatin and juices. Mix and pour into freezer bags. Freeze overnight. To serve, partially thaw punch and add 2 liters of Canada Dry® Ginger Ale. Makes about 40 servings.

Twist and Shout Punch

1 46-ounce can pineapple juice

3 packages instant cherry-flavored drink mix
   (prepared as instructed)

1 2-liter bottle Canada Dry® Ginger Ale

sugar to taste

3–6 lemons, sliced

Mix pineapple juice and cherry drink. Chill. When ready to serve, add Canada Dry® Ginger Ale and sugar to taste. Garnish with lemon slices. Makes about 28 servings.

Happy Holidays Punch

juice of 3 lemons
juice of 6 oranges
¾ cup pineapple juice
¾ cup powdered sugar
1 liter Canada Dry® Ginger Ale
lemon slices
orange slices
ice

Combine first five ingredients in large punch bowl and stir gently. Add fresh fruit slices and ice to top of punch and stir. Makes 18 servings.

Wink and a Smile Punch

2 cups water
2 cups sugar
1 3-ounce package of strawberry gelatin
1 quart nonalcoholic pink champagne
1 quart pineapple juice
1 teaspoon almond extract
½ cup lemon juice
1 2-liter bottle 7 UP®
ice

Boil water and sugar. Add gelatin and stir until dissolved. Combine with next five ingredients and serve in punch bowl over ice. Makes about 20 servings.

Crazy Uncle Kurt's Fruity Punch

1 ½ cups sugar

3 cups water

1 ½ cups pineapple juice

1 6-ounce can frozen orange juice concentrate,
    thawed

3 bananas, mashed

3 tablespoons lemon juice

1 liter Canada Dry® Ginger Ale

ice

orange slices

lemon slices

Combine sugar, water, pineapple, and orange juice. Blend bananas and lemon juice and mix with sugar and liquids. Freeze for 1–2 days before serving. Just before serving, add Canada Dry® Ginger Ale and ice. Garnish with orange and lemon slices. Makes about 20 servings.

Raspberry Delight Punch

1 cup sugar
1 cup water
juice of 3 lemons
3 cups iced tea
1 cup fresh or frozen raspberries, thawed
¾ cup crushed pineapple
ice
1 quart Canada Dry® Ginger Ale

Bring sugar and water to boil until sugar is dissolved. Combine water with lemon juice and tea. Place raspberries and pineapple in large punch bowl over ice. Pour tea mixture over fruit and ice. And add chilled Canada Dry® Ginger Ale. Makes about 18 servings.

Very Cherry Punch

3 packages instant cherry-flavored drink mix
3 quarts water
3 cups sugar
1 46-ounce can pineapple juice
1 quart Canada Dry® Ginger Ale
maraschino cherries

Mix first five ingredients and chill. Garnish with maraschino cherries. Makes about 40 servings.

Punch Line Punch

1 12-ounce can frozen orange juice
8 cups water
4 cups cranberry juice
¾ cup sugar
orange slices

Mix first four ingredients and chill. Pour into large punch bowl. Garnish with orange slices. Makes about 28 servings.

Peach Punch

1 ½ cups peach nectar
2 cups water
1 cup sugar
1 46-ounce can pineapple juice
1 liter Canada Dry® Ginger Ale
ice
lemon slices

Mix first five ingredients together until sugar is dissolved. Pour into large punch bowl. Add ice and lemon slices. Makes 28 servings.

CHAPTER

9

Hot Punches for Cool Occasions

For those occasions that call for a warm drink for a large number of guests, try one of these new varieties of favorite warm punches. Remember that cinnamon sticks and flavored candy canes are always a fun way to spice up a warm cup.

Spice Island Tea

- 3 quarts boiling water
- 1 cup sugar
- 1 lemon, juiced
- 1 tablespoon grated lemon rind
- 2 oranges, juiced
- 1 tablespoon grated orange rind
- 2 teaspoons whole cloves
- 4 cinnamon sticks
- 1 ½ tablespoons instant tea
- lemon slices

Combine first nine ingredients in a large pot and simmer over medium heat for about 20–25 minutes. Strain. Serve hot in mugs. Garnish with lemon slices. Makes 25 servings.

Hot Cranberry Punch

1 16-ounce can jellied cranberry sauce
⅓ cup brown sugar, packed
¼ teaspoon ground cinnamon
¼ teaspoon ground allspice
⅛ teaspoon ground cloves
⅛ teaspoon ground nutmeg
2 cups water
2 cups pineapple juice
cinnamon sticks

Crush cranberry sauce with fork. Mix with sugar and spices. Add water and pineapple juice. Cover and simmer on stove top for about 2 hours. Serve in mugs with cinnamon sticks. Makes 8–10 servings.

Spicy Cranberry Cider

2 oranges, sliced
8 cups MOTT'S® apple juice
3 cups cranberry juice
1 teaspoon whole cloves
1 teaspoon allspice
8 cinnamon sticks
2 cups hot tea

Set aside 1 sliced orange for garnish. Combine all other ingredients in large saucepan. Heat and simmer about 30 minutes. Serve warm in mugs with orange slices to garnish. Makes about 20 servings.

Spiced Cider Bowl

  4 cups cranberry juice
  3 cups MOTT'S® apple juice
  ¼ cup sugar
  2 cinnamon sticks
  16 whole cloves
  2 oranges, sliced

Combine cranberry juice, MOTT'S® apple juice, sugar, cinnamon, and cloves in a large pot. Slice oranges and add some to pot. Stir gently and simmer 15–20 minutes. Pour into warmed punch bowl and garnish with orange slices. Makes 18 servings.

Rum Coffee Punch

  12 cups strong black coffee
  ¼ cup sugar
  ¾ cup half and half
  2 tablespoon rum flavoring

Prepare coffee. Add sugar while coffee is still hot. Let cool. Then add cream and rum. Beat with electric mixer on low. Before serving, bring to a boil and serve hot. Makes 12 servings.

Good Golly Miss Molly Punch

1 ½ cups sugar
2 cups water
1 cup pineapple juice
2 cups cranberry juice
2 cups orange juice
1 cup lemon juice
4 cups water
lemon slices

Combine first seven ingredients. Heat and simmer about 15 minutes. Serve hot in mugs. Garnish with lemon slice. Makes 12 servings.

Hot Wassail Tea

1 6-ounce can frozen orange juice concentrate, thawed
1 6-ounce can frozen lemonade concentrate, thawed
1 quart MOTT'S® apple juice
1 cup sugar
1 ½ teaspoons whole cloves
3 cinnamon sticks
1 teaspoon ground ginger
5 cups hot water
3 cups strong tea
20 cinnamon sticks

Mix juices in large pot. Add sugar and spices and warm over medium heat. Slowly add water and tea. Simmer for about 15 minutes and serve hot in mugs. Garnish with cinnamon sticks. Makes 20 servings.

Cappuccino

    3 cinnamon sticks
    1 tablespoon whole cloves
    ½ cup instant coffee
    ½ cup sugar
    6 cups boiling water
    3 cups half & half, warmed
    2 cups whipped cream
    nutmeg

Tie cinnamon sticks and cloves in cheesecloth. Place in large pot. Add coffee and sugar. Pour in boiling water to dissolve. Cover and steep 5 minutes. Remove spice bag. Add half & half. Serve in warm mugs and top with whipped cream. Sprinkle with nutmeg. Makes 16 servings.

The Jolly Dutchman

½ cup sugar
½ cup boiling water
17 cinnamon sticks
1 teaspoon whole cloves
2 quarts MOTT'S® apple juice
2 cups orange juice
½ cup lemon juice

Dissolve sugar in boiling water in saucepan. Tie 3 cinnamon sticks and 1 teaspoon whole cloves in cheesecloth. Add juices and spice bag to water and heat to medium heat. Simmer about 20 minutes. Remove spice bag and serve beverage hot in mugs with cinnamon sticks to garnish. Makes about 14 servings.

Spicy Peach Punch

½ cup boiling water
⅓ cup sugar
1 ½ quarts peach nectar
1 quart orange juice
4 cinnamon sticks
1 teaspoon whole cloves
3 tablespoons lemon juice

Boil water and sugar in saucepan until sugar dissolves. Add the other ingredients. Heat slowly. Just before serving, remove cloves and cinnamon sticks with slotted spoon. Makes 12–16 servings.

Hot Cocoa Punch

1 ¼ cups cocoa
1 ½ cups sugar
½ teapoon salt
2 cups cold water
1 gallon hot milk
¾ teaspoon vanilla
marshmallow cream
chocolate shavings

Combine cocoa, sugar, and salt in pot. Mix well. Add water and stir. Bring to a boil. Add hot milk and vanilla. Stir. Serve in mugs. Top with marshmallow cream and chocolate shavings. Makes 26 servings.

Minty Chocolate Punch

    3 quarts hot water
    1 quart hot milk
    1 ½ cups hot cocoa mix
    ⅛ cup peppermint flavoring
    24 candy canes

Simmer water and milk over medium heat for about 10–15 minutes. Add hot cocoa mix and peppermint flavoring. Stir until well mixed. Let simmer another 5–10 minutes, stirring occasionally. Serve in mugs. Garnish with candy canes. Makes about 24 servings.

CHAPTER

10

Theme Party Punches

A re you hosting an office party, wedding shower, or family get-together? Jazz it up with a creative theme. Invite your guests to show up in grass skirts, display their favorite sports team jerseys, or dress as their favorite politicians. Go crazy with the theme and make sure your punch rises to the occasion.

Hawaii 5-0 Punch

(Perfect for a Hawaiian luau)
    2 quarts pineapple juice
    1 liter Cherry 7 UP®
    ¾ cup lemon juice
    2 quarts pineapple sherbet
    maraschino cherries

Combine first four ingredients in large bowl and beat with electric mixer on low until sherbet is slightly melted and creamy. Serve immediately. Garnish with maraschino cherries. Makes 16 servings.

Aloha Punch

(Another natural for a luau. Ask your guests to dress Hawaiian!)
    3 quarts pineapple juice
    juice of 8 lemons
    juice of 8 oranges
        ½ cup sugar
        1 cup fresh mint leaves
        2 2-liter bottles 7 UP®
        1 pint fresh strawberries, quartered
        ice ring or crushed ice
        lemon or lime slices

Combine fruit juices, sugar, and mint leaves. Chill. Just before serving, add 7 UP® and strawberries. Pour over ice ring or crushed ice. Add lemon or lime slices. Makes about 60 servings.

The Big Dipper

(Ask your guests to bring their favorite chips and dips.
You provide the beverages.)

> 2 2-liter bottles Canada Dry® Ginger Ale
> maraschino cherries
> 1 12-ounce can frozen limeade concentrate, thawed
> 1 12-ounce can frozen lemonade concentrate,
>   thawed
> fresh lime slices
> green food coloring, optional

Pour Canada Dry® Ginger Ale into 4 ice cube trays. Add
a maraschino cherry to each cube. Freeze overnight. In
punch bowl, combine limeade and lemonade concen-
trates and remaining Canada Dry® Ginger Ale. Add 2
trays of frozen Canada Dry® Ginger Ale cubes and lime
slices. Tint a pale green, if desired. Add remaining frozen
Canada Dry® Ginger Ale cubes as needed. Makes about
22 servings.

Wedding Shower Punch

4 cups orange juice
4 cups MOTT'S® apple juice
ice
4 cups Canada Dry® Ginger Ale
orange slices

Mix orange juice and MOTT'S® apple juice in punch bowl with ice. Add Canada Dry® Ginger Ale and stir gently. Garnish with orange slices. Makes 12 servings.

Summer Shower Punch

2 6-ounce cans frozen grape juice, thawed
4 6-ounce cans frozen orange juice concentrate, thawed
1 liter chilled Canada Dry® Ginger Ale
2 cups pineapple juice
7 6-ounce cans of water
16 scoops lime sherbet

Combine first five ingredients in large punch bowl. Serve in tall glasses with a scoop of lime sherbet. Makes 16 servings.

Political Party Punch

(Great around election time. Invite your guests to dress like their favorite politicians.)

    1 pint cranberry juice
    2 cups pineapple juice
    ½ cup water
    ⅓ cup brown sugar
    ½ teaspoon whole cloves
    ½ teaspoon allspice
    3 cinnamon sticks
    4 cinnamon sticks for garnish

Combine juices, water, and brown sugar in percolator. Place spices in basket. Perk. Serve in mugs with cinnamon sticks to garnish. Makes 4 servings.

Solid Gold Punch

(Great for Oscar night! Make it a first-class evening and require black-tie attire.)

    2 quarts cold water
    1 cup sugar
    1 teaspoon vanilla
    2 6-ounce cans frozen orange juice concentrate,
        thawed
    1 46-ounce can pineapple juice
    2 6-ounce cans frozen lemonade concentrate,
        thawed
    crushed ice
    orange slices
    mint sprigs

Heat water to boiling. Add sugar and stir until sugar is dissolved. Let cool. Add vanilla, juices, and lemonade. Pour mixture into punch bowl over ice. Garnish with orange slices and mint sprigs. Makes about 20 servings

Pretty in Pink Punch

(Just for fun. Require that your guests wear something pink.)

 1 6-ounce package strawberry gelatin
 1 cup boiling water
 1 cup cold water
 1 46-ounce can pineapple juice
 1 cup crushed pineapple
 ice
 1 2-liter bottle Canada Dry® Sparkling Water
 fresh strawberries

Combine first 3 ingredients and stir until well mixed. Add juice and pineapple. Mix well and freeze overnight. About 3 hours before serving time, move to refrigerator. When ready to serve, place in punch bowl over ice and add Canada Dry® Sparkling Water. Garnish with fresh strawberries. Makes about 32 servings.

Party of Five Punch

(Invite your friends over on your favorite TV night.)
- 4 ripe bananas
- 1 cup sugar
- 3 ¼ cups water
- 1 6-ounce can frozen orange juice concentrate, thawed
- 1 46-ounce can pineapple juice
- 1 6-ounce can lemonade concentrate, thawed
- 2 packages cherry-flavored drink mix.
- 1 quart Canada Dry® Ginger Ale

Blend bananas, sugar, and water. Mix with juices and drink mix. Freeze until slushy. Add Canada Dry® Ginger Ale at serving time. Makes about 26 servings.

Alice in Wonderland Punch

(Perfect for a "Mad Hatter" party. Guests must come wearing their favorite hats.)
- 1 12-ounce package strawberry gelatin
- 2 cups boiling water
- 6 cups cold water
- 1 46-ounce can pineapple juice
- 1 12-ounce can frozen orange juice
- ice
- 1 2-liter bottle Canada Dry® Ginger Ale

Dissolve gelatin in 2 cups boiling water. Stir in cold water and chill. Add pineapple juice and orange juice and chill. Combine all ingredients in punch bowl over ice and slowly stir in Canada Dry® Ginger Ale. Makes about 40 servings.

Oktoberfest Punch

2 pounds frozen strawberries, thawed
½ cup sugar
2 bottles nonalcoholic white wine
1 2-liter bottle Canada Dry® Club Soda
ice

Place strawberries in punch bowl and sprinkle with ½ cup sugar. Cover with 1 bottle nonalcoholic white wine. Chill. When ready to serve, add second bottle of nonalcoholic white wine and 2 liters of Canada Dry® Club Soda and ice. Makes 20 servings.

Hot Fun in the Summertime

(Great for a casual poolside summer celebration.)
1 package instant cherry-flavored drink mix
1 package instant strawberry-flavored drink mix
2 cups sugar
2 quarts cold water
1 6-ounce can frozen orange juice concentrate, thawed
1 6-ounce can frozen lemonade concentrate, thawed
4 cups crushed ice
1 liter Canada Dry® Ginger Ale
lemon slices

Combine powdered drink mixes with sugar and water. Stir until dissolved. Add juices. Chill until serving time. Place ice in punch bowl and slowly add juice mixture over ice. Add Canada Dry® Ginger Ale and lemon slices. Makes 16 servings.

Grand Slam Punch

(Invite your friends to watch the World Series, Super Bowl, or other sporting events. Ask them to wear their favorite team jerseys.)

    1 2-liter bottle 7 UP® chilled
    2 pints cranberry juice
    1 quart MOTT'S® apple juice
    lemon slices

Pour 7 UP® in two ice cube trays. Freeze. At serving time, place 7 UP® cubes in punch bowl and add cranberry juice and MOTT'S® apple juice. Slowly pour in rest of 7 UP®. Garnish with lemon slices. Makes 10–12 servings.

CHAPTER

11

Fun Drinks Just For Kids

For parents of small children, these fun drinks may just give you that extra little bit of color you've been looking for to brighten up a day. They can also be the surprise kick to make a birthday party a huge success.

Polka Dot Punch

12 jelly beans
5 cups pineapple juice
6 cups orange juice
4 cups MOTT'S® apple juice

Place one jelly bean in each cube in an ice cube tray. Pour pineapple juice to fill tray and freeze overnight. Mix orange juice, MOTT'S® apple juice, and remaining pineapple juice in punch bowl. Before serving, add jelly bean ice cubes and serve chilled. Makes about 28 servings.

Birthday Party Punch

3 packages instant drink mix—any flavor
3 quarts water
3 cups sugar
3 cups pineapple juice
1 2-liter bottle Canada Dry® Ginger Ale
ice

Combine all ingredients in a punch bowl over ice. Makes about 30 servings.

Colorful Hot Chocolate

3 tablespoons hot cocoa mix
¼ cup milk
½ cup hot water
colored marshmallows

In a mug, combine cocoa mix and milk. Slowly stir in hot water. Top with colored marshmallows. Makes 1 serving.

Icy Grape Juice Treat

2 cups crushed ice
¾ cup grape juice
1 cup 7 UP®
¼ cup MOTT'S® apple juice

Combine all ingredients in blender. Mix until blended well. Makes 2 servings.

Lemonade Icy

2 cups lemonade
1 cup 7 UP®
2 cups crushed ice
fresh strawberries

Combine first three ingredients and blend until slushy. Garnish with fresh strawberry. Makes 2–4 servings.

Homemade Mini Popsicles

fruit juices, any flavor

Pour fruit juice in an ice cube tray. Place 1 toothpick in each cube. Freeze overnight. Makes 12 popsicles per tray.

Colorful Sparkle

½ cup ice
1 cup 7 UP®
food coloring (child's choice)
jelly beans

Place ½ cup ice in glass. Fill glass with 7 UP®. Add 4–5 drops food coloring and stir. Top with jelly beans. Makes 1 serving.

Rainbow Float

1 scoop rainbow sherbet
2 cups 7 UP®
candy sprinkles

Place 1 scoop sherbet in parfait glass. Fill with 7 UP®. Sprinkle candies on top to garnish. Makes 1 serving.

Peanut Butter Shake

   3 scoops vanilla ice cream
   1 tablespoon creamy peanut butter
   2 tablespoons chocolate syrup
   ½ cup milk

Combine all ingredients in blender and blend until smooth. Serve immediately. Makes 2 servings.

Purple People Eater Float

   3 scoops vanilla ice cream
   1 cup grape juice
   1 cup Canada Dry® Ginger Ale
   1 tablespoon milk

Combine 2 scoops ice cream, grape juice, Canada Dry® Ginger Ale, and milk in blender. Mix until blended. Place 1 scoop of ice cream in chilled glass and fill glass with grape drink. Makes 1 serving.

Orange You Glad I Didn't Say Banana Float

   1 ½ cups Sunkist® Orange Soda
   1 ½ cups Canada Dry® Ginger Ale
   2 scoops orange sherbet

Combine Sunkist® Orange and Canada Dry® Ginger Ale. Place 1 scoop orange sherbet in each of two chilled glasses and fill glasses with soda mixture. Makes 2 servings.

Grape Sparkle Float

 1 ½ cups grape juice
 1 ½ cups 7 UP®
 2 scoops vanilla ice cream

Combine grape juice and 7 UP®. Place one scoop vanilla ice cream in each of two chilled glasses and fill with soda mixture. Makes 2 servings.

Somewhere over the Rainbow Punch

 1 quart fruit punch
 1 quart orange juice
 2 cups pineapple juice
 4 cups MOTT'S® apple juice
 1 tablespoon lemon juice

Pour fruit punch into ice cube trays and freeze overnight. Mix other juices together in punch bowl and stir until well blended. Chill. When ready to serve, add fruit punch ice cubes. Makes about 10 servings.